Mr. Mauna Kea

Mr. Mauna Kea

Adi W. Kohler

Catherine Bridges Tarleton

McKenna Publishing Group

Indian Wells, California

Mr. Mauna Kea

ISBN: 1-932172-16-5
LCCN: 2003114661

Cover design by Leslie Parker

First Edition
10 9 8 7 6 5 4 3 2 1
Printed in the United States of America

Visit us on the Web at: www.mckennapubgrp.com

Acknowledgements

We would like to thank the following individuals for their essential help in the creation of *Mr. Mauna Kea*. Their contribution of information, connection to other sources, editorial assistance and encouraging words are more valuable than they know. There are many others, and it would be impossible to name each person who added their thoughts and *aloha,* including past and present employees of Mauna Kea Beach Hotel, whose good work continues to build her history as a very special place on Earth.

John Black

Ric Bollinger

Robert Butterfield

Patti Cook

Ray Corliss

Celeste Dudley

W. Clayton Frye, Jr.

Jeremiah Gruenberg

Chaz Hendrickson

Robert Itamoto

Ulrike "Bieni" Johnson

Frank Morgan

Leslie Parker

Keoki Pelfrey

Laurance S. Rockefeller

David Shackleton

Steve Shalit

Dwight Tarleton

For Chacha (Kathrin), Bieni (Ulrike), Christian (Tiger),
Alicia, Ryan, Elyse and Alexander (Adi)

PROLOGUE

"Let me show you around," said Adi Kohler, General Manager of Mauna Kea Beach Hotel. The introductory talk with the new Assistant GM was over and it was time for a property tour. Kohler walked around his big koa wood desk to escort him out, but the new Assistant was stopped by the view, staring out at the sparkling ocean.

"How do you get any work done?" he asked.

Kohler laughed and patted him on the shoulder. "That's the secret, Tom," he said. "It's not work. It's fun." He buttoned his white suit jacket, smoothed the front.

"I'll try to remember that." Tom Scott stood, pulling his gaze away from the window, glad he'd listened to his wife and had worn the sportcoat.

One wall of the Executive Office was ocean window; the other three were nearly full of photos and awards. A decorated ribbon from the Confrérie de la Chaîne des Rôtisseurs, designated Kohler Bailli (President) and founder of the Big Island chapter. Certificates named him President of the Hawaii Hotel Association, another Big Island first, and the 1988 Resort Executive of the Year from the American Hotel & Motel Association. There were commendations from the Mayor, the Governor, the Chamber of Commerce, and thank-you plaques from local and mainland charity organizations. In the corner was a large custom golf bag, bright green and white, which read, "To Adi from Chi Chi."

Down the hall were Mauna Kea's years of AAA Five-diamond Awards, its Honor Award from the American Institute of Architects, accolades from *Condé Nast, Esquire, Travel & Leisure, Golf Digest* and many other travel publications and organizations. Shelves filled with trophies and commemorative gifts made it hard to distinguish his from the hotel's. There were many photos, Kohler with the Emperor of Japan, Kohler with Laurance S. Rockefeller. One picture showed him on horseback with a long cavalcade of Western riders. Nearby hung a leather lanyard, branded "El Campo De Los Bustardos."

"What's this?" said the new Assistant.

"Oh that's a little ride I take every year," said Kohler. "With *mi compadres* in the Rancheros Visitadores."

"The what?"

"That's somewhat of a longer story than we have time for right now."

On the way out, the new Assistant pointed to a framed black and white print on the back of the door. "What about this one?" he asked.

"That's the village where my brother lives, in Germany."

"Is that where you're from?"

"No," said Kohler. "The place I was born was called Sudetenland. Right now, it's more or less part of the Czech Republic."

"So you're Czech?" said the new Assistant.

Kohler smiled again, broadly. "I'm an American, brother," he said. "But I call myself a former European." He was anxious to get going, glanced at his watch. "Let's go. We have a lot of ground to cover."

"But how did you get here?"

"That is another long story," said Kohler. "Which we will get into over dinner, maybe. Come on."

The two of them walked down the back corridor and through the Accounting Office where everyone stopped to be introduced and say hello. Accounting was key to the new Assistant orientation process. Most of the ladies had been working there for many years and were ultimately warm and hospitable. More importantly, they were quick at sizing a person up. By the time Kohler and the new Assistant reached the next department, the staff would know what he looked like. In half an hour, his description would be hotel-wide. By 5:00, the incoming nightshift would already know who he was and the next day he'd be part of the family. This lightning-style gossip was called the "coconut wireless" and worked more efficiently to pass on information than computer technology could ever hope to.

The Controller came out of his office to say hello. He checked the clock on the wall against his Rolex. "Welcome aboard, Tom," he said. "Morning Adi." He and Kohler went back a number of years. They remembered days when the Controller's job was quite different, when money wasn't exactly a non-issue, but it wasn't the only issue. Not when you worked for Rockresorts. Mr. Rockefeller used to say, "If you don't think of money, you make it as a by-product or you don't. But if you don't, you're not aware of it; if you do, it's a surprise." In other words, perhaps, profit should not be more important than quality, but rather be a natural, pleasant outcome of it. These conversations usually happened closer to the bottom of a bottle of wine.

Kohler and the new Assistant continued down the corridor, past even more certificates, magazine covers and award-winning ad campaigns. They waved at the Director of Sales, who placed his phone call on hold to say hello. He offered to show Mr. Scott the marketing plan for the present year and his group sales strategies for the next. The new Assistant said he'd call, as soon as he had a telephone.

They stepped outside into a garden area, koi ponds on both sides of a shaded atrium walkway. "Let's start at the Front Desk." Kohler walked briskly, gesturing with his left hand. "Below is the Copper Bar and the Terrace restaurant where we serve the buffet for lunch every day and Sunday Brunch. The Batik is to the left. We'll have dinner there tonight. These are our koi carp, keeping themselves busy." He greeted a groundskeeper, carefully netting leaves off the surface of the pond. They walked between the fishponds and went up a few steps, past an imposing Japanese calligraphy painting in black and gold.

"What's that?" asked the new Assistant.

"Part of the art collection. We have more than 1600 pieces all over the hotel. That one says, 'a dragon knows a dragon.'"

"What does that mean?"

There was a noise from the Front Desk. Loud voices. Kohler moved in that direction. The new Assistant followed.

A lady guest jangled her keys at the Desk Clerk, then slammed them down on the counter. "I will not stay in 602," she said.

From the floor below the Lobby, a raucous voice squawked out "Aloha!"

"I'm sorry, Mrs. Johnson," said Alvin, from behind the Desk. "Is there something wrong with your room?"

"What was that?" said the new Assistant.

"That's Aleka," said Kohler. "He's our parrot."

"It's not my room. It's blue!" she said. "We've been coming here for fourteen years and I always have a yellow room with twin beds facing the ocean. We have never stayed in a blue room and I am not going to stay in a blue room tonight. It is not acceptable and I want to know what you're going to do about it."

Aleka got louder as she did, "Aloha! Aloha!"

"I'm sorry," said Alvin. "I can understand why you're upset."

"You haven't seen me upset yet, young man," said the guest. "I want my yellow room and I want it right now."

"Let me get the Manager on Duty for you, Mrs. Johnson."

The new Assistant looked over the rail to see a bright-colored Scarlet Macaw hanging from the bars of a huge brass cage. He flapped his wings and let out a blood-curdling screech.

"I don't want the Manager on Duty. I want to speak with Adi Kohler. Where is Adi Kohler?"

"ALOHA, ALOHA, ALOHA!"

"He's right behind you, Mrs. Johnson."

The guest slowly turned around, holding on to her attitude as best she could. Kohler smiled, extended his hand.

"Mrs. Johnson," he said. "What have we done to you?"

"I want my room," she said.

Below, one of the gift shop girls came out to give Aleka a macadamia nut. He decided to take a break.

"I'm sorry, Mr. Kohler," said Alvin. "It's the only Ocean View we have available."

Kohler smiled at the distraught Mrs. Johnson. "Of course you want your room," he said. He guided her over to a chair away from the others, and spoke to her slowly and soothingly, gradually toning the conversation down to a manageable level. "Now Mrs. Johnson," he said. "You know we can make 602 a yellow room like *that*." He snapped his fingers. "All I have to do is call Housekeeping. What's the real problem?"

She sniffed back tears. "My ex-husband is right next door," she said, "with that bimbo he married." She started to cry in earnest. Kohler waved Alvin over with tissues. She blew her nose. "I wanted this to be a special place for me and my husband, my new husband. And that bad man, that bastard has ruined everything. I want to go home."

"Give me a moment, Mrs. Johnson."

Kohler, the new Assistant and Alvin conferred in the back. It was true. The ex had arrived with his new wife but their room, 604, wasn't ready yet, so they'd gone down to breakfast. Possibly snooping, Mrs. Johnson saw the name on their luggage tags and went into hysterics. Her present husband retreated to the Copper Bar. "Move the ex," Kohler said to Alvin.

"Where?"

"Find him a room. I know Jack and I know he will kill me if he ends up next door to her."

"You can have my room," said the new Assistant. "Put him in there and put me anywhere."

"Now you're thinking, brother." Kohler slapped him on the back. "What room is he in?"

"810," said Alvin. "But it's a check-out. I can't get it ready till late this afternoon."

"Do it Alvin, and I'll call Housekeeping to get the beds changed out and the yellow spreads."

"And the Sexton print," said Alvin. "Be sure they switch the Morning Glory for the Shower Tree. I'll change the folios."

"Right." Kohler picked up the phone. In a few minutes, the switch was done and champagne was ordered for 602 and 810, just to be safe.

Mrs. Johnson gave him a damp hug. "Oh thank you, Adi," she said.

"It's our pleasure, Mrs. Johnson." He looked at Alvin. "It's only too bad we didn't have everything in order before you arrived." She went off to find her present husband.

"I'm sorry, Mr. Kohler. I'll make sure all this is in her file. Yellow room. Ex-husband and bimbo." He smiled. "Welcome to Mauna Kea, Mr. Scott."

"Thank you, Alvin."

Kohler said, "Get the guest history straightened out and we won't have to go through this with her the next time." He led the new Assistant to a wood railing that overlooked the vast ocean. Kohler stroked the glossy finish, then frowned at the palm of his hand.

"Whew," said the new Assistant.

"Oh, that was an easy one," said Kohler. "Besides it's good for business."

"Beg your pardon?"

"Sure," said Kohler. "They get married and come to Mauna Kea. Then they have kids and bring them to Mauna Kea. Next thing you know they get divorced and come to Mauna Kea with the new spouses and their kids, and so on and so forth."

"Like a pyramid scheme."

"Something like that. But more interesting. Besides, what they do with their life is their business. All we have to do is take care of them once they are here. That's our job. Simple."

The new Assistant turned around and looked toward the Front Circle. He watched a couple of arriving guests receive their plumeria *lei* and step between the shining gold *mokala* statues, their hands folded in a gesture of welcome. The guests smiled up at the three tall coconut palms reaching up through the open atrium. He followed their gaze upward. "What do you do when it rains?" he asked.

Kohler nodded at Alvin, who pressed a control button. "Someone asked Mr. Rockefeller the same question," said Kohler, "so he did this." Glass panels in the ceiling slid out of their recess pockets and closed in the lobby, just brushing the tips of the palm fronds. "Do something about the things you can do something about," he said. "I can't stop the rain; I'm not in charge of the weather. But we can close the skylight, and everybody's more or less happy." He started walking again. "Sooner or later we'll have to cut them down, I guess," he said, "whenever they get too tall for the ceiling."

They headed left, past a little garden filled with chattering birds in ornate cages, to the Real Estate Office, where Kohler introduced him to the agents. "And this is Chacha," he said. "My wife and my strong right arm." A smiling blonde woman stood up to greet the new Assistant.

"How nice to finally meet you, Tom," she said. "You're joining us for dinner tonight?"

"Of course he is," said Kohler.

"And your wife?"

"She'll be here on Sunday," said the new Assistant.

Chacha outside the Mauna Kea Realty office

"Good then," said Chacha. "She's part of the family, you know."

"That's what I understand."

"Everybody thinks it's the man with the job title who does all the work," said Chacha. "But it takes both to keep the guests entertained."

"That's right."

"Because they are mostly couples and they like socializing with other couples, especially happy couples. That's the way it works. It takes two."

"Now don't lecture the man, Schatzi," said Kohler. "He's only just arrived."

"What about children?" she said.

"We don't have kids."

"You will," she said. "All of our assistant managers have babies here."

"They do?"

"Oh yes," she said. "It's a tradition."

The Kohlers laughed. They were the welcoming committee and the official host and hostess of the Mauna Kea Beach Hotel. The guests were their friends, and they enjoyed each other's company as part of an ever-expanding social circle, one that rotated continuously, bringing them back together year after year. Mr. Rockefeller said that "Adi and Chacha were a great team, one of the reasons the Mauna Kea was able to communicate the great spirit of aloha that was felt by guests and staff alike."

Kohler continued the tour, showing his new Assistant how to steal a cookie from the pastry shop, then walked through the dining room as the late breakfast crowd was finishing their coffee.

"Mr. Kohler," said one of the guests as they passed. He stood up to shake his hand. "I understand you saved my neck. Thank you."

"No problem, Jack," said Kohler. "But your room's not going to be ready till late this afternoon. Why don't you go ahead out on the golf course and enjoy yourself? Is this your lovely lady?"

A gorgeous blonde offered her diamond-clad hand and gave him a very expensive smile. "Tiffany," she said.

Later, the new Assistant asked, "Was that her name or the ring?"

Kohler laughed. "I was afraid to ask."

At the far end of the building, off the loading dock, they found the Director of Engineering in his office, nearly buried by catalogues, drawings and blueprints. He was a small man with a big heart, always running, but never too busy to talk with the boss, answer his questions and listen to his concerns. And fix it if he could. Today it was the wooden railings in the Lobby.

"They're turning black again," Kohler said. "Isn't there something you can put on it? It looks ugly."

The Director of Engineering went into a lengthy explanation of the properties of *narra* wood from the Philippines, how it was designed to be unfinished to give it a natural look, but a new product he was experimenting with called sea-fin oil was supposed to protect the wood from the salt and moisture content of the air, however it had to be applied in layers in gradual stages because...

"I'm sure you know what you're talking about," said Kohler. He slapped him on the shoulder and left him to work. As they walked toward the *lu'au* grounds, the new Assistant asked a question. "Do you want me to write him a m emo about the railing project?'"

"You saw his office," said Kohler with a smile. He picked up a candy wrapper from the grass. "A memo wouldn't stand a chance in there."

"Well then how do you want me to follow up with him?"

"Leave him alone. Let him do his job."

"Just like that?"

"When you hire the best people for the job, you have to trust them to get it done."

The tour went on and on, through the Tennis Park, the Property Services Office and the North Garden, where the new Assistant met the Buddha, and rubbed his belly for good luck. They walked along the roadway to the Golf Pro Shop and after introductions all around, went to lunch at the 19th Hole.

"Aloha Mr. Kohler," said a chorus of smiling waitresses. "Welcome to the Mauna Kea, Mr. Scott." Their table was ready. Kohler ordered his usual fish; the new Assistant had a club sandwich. The waitresses fluttered and fussed over them like aunties, bringing extra rolls and keeping the water glasses full. An incoming tableful of guests stopped by to say hello.

Kohler picked up his bread and started tearing it into bites. "Tell me a little about yourself," he said. This was the signal for the new Assistan to talk, which he did for about five minutes until Kohler had finished eating.

"You eat fast," he said.

"Bad habit," said Kohler. "I spent too many years in the restaurant business. We never had time to sit and eat, so I never learned how to do that." He placed his fork across the top edge of the plate, laid his napkin on the table. "Now, what are your questions so far?" A waitress removed the plate and offered coffee or decaffeinated. Having dispensed with lunch, Kohler now gave full attention to answers both entertaining and educational. When the new Assistant finished his sandwich and refused dessert, Kohler pulled a Cross pen out of his pocket and signed the check with green ink. "Let's take a look at the golf course."

The boys had cart #1 ready for their tour. As they pulled away from the first tee, Kohler spotted a wayward ball and retrieved it from the edge of the rough.

"Do you play golf?" said Kohler.

"Not as well as I'd like to," he said. "I guess you play all the time."

"I'm still learning," said Kohler. "When I started out at Mauna Kea, my handicap was 26, then it steadily improved and now I'm a 32!"

The new Assistant couldn't keep his head from turning back-and-forth to take it all in. Everywhere he looked was a view more dazzling than the last. They stopped at Number Three. "You have to hit it from here?" said the new Assistant. "Across the ocean?" He watched a wave surge into the little inlet between the tee and the green, crash white against the black lava. "Wow."

"Wow is right," said Kohler. "At Christmas time, we do what we call a 'champagne shoot-out.' After a couple glasses of champagne, we let them try for a hole-in-one. If anybody makes it, we give them a night on the house."

"Have you ever had to pay up?"

"Once or twice," said Kohler. "The guests love it."

"Have you ever hit it?"

"A hole-in-one?" Kohler laughed. "From here? You must be dreaming. I'll never do that in my life."

They continued up the fourth fairway, then cut across to the entry road and turned off into the private estate subdivision of the Fairways North, custom homes built for those guests who wanted to make the Mauna Kea lifestyle their own. "Wow," said the new Assistant. "These are incredible. I wonder if I'll ever be able to afford something like this."

"Not on your salary, brother," said Kohler. "We have another group at the Fairways South, and the Villas are condominium units down below."

"Those are the ones you can see from the Pro Shop?"

"That's right."

"These are the properties your wife sells?"

"That's right, and she does it extremely well," he said. "She makes more money than I do!"

They hopped back onto the cart path and drove up to a higher elevation. Kohler stopped by the tenth tee and retrieved another lost ball. The Golf Course Superintendent was digging in the grass with his pocket knife. They stopped the cart.

"Still fighting the war with the weeds, Mr. Kohler," said the man. He tossed the clump of crabgrass into the back of his cart, and wiped his hand on his pantleg. "You must be the new Assistant. I'm Bob Itamoto." They shook hands. "I promised Mr. Rockefeller 98% weeds free in 1964," he said. "So far, so good."

"You're doing a beautiful job," said the new Assistant.

"Wait until you get the chance the play. You're going to love it."

"I know. I can hardly wait."

"See you later, Bob," said Kohler. "We have a lot of ground to cover."

They dropped onto the beach access road just off the eighteenth hole, where Mrs. Johnson's ex-husband, minus bimbo, was finishing up his round. They pulled into the driveway of a separate cottage on a little knoll above the beach. A man in aloha shirt came out to greet them. "Hello, Bill," said Kohler.

He shook the new Assistant's hand. "Bill Mielcke," he said. "Welcome aboard."

"Now this is an office," said the new Assistant.

Mielcke smiled. "It's doesn't get much better than this, does it?"

"Bill is president of our land company," said Kohler, "in charge of all the development projects we have going on."

"Development projects?"

Mielcke gestured with his left hand, down the coast. "We're looking right now at the land between here and Hapuna Beach. If we can work everything out with the County, we can start work on the second golf course and the next phase of residential properties. We're making progress."

"Wow," said the new Assistant.

"You're saying that a lot," said Kohler.

"It's just so much more than I expected."

"Don't get used to it. Everything changes, brother. That's the one thing we know for sure." He looked down the beach where Mielcke pointed. "Everything changes."

"Let me know if I can help with anything," said Mielcke.

"I'll do that," said the new Assistant.

They took the cart to a wide green lawn overlooking the ocean, where a bustling team of banquet porters was setting up chairs and tables. Blue-shirted engineers were up in the trees, running strings of lights while another group laid down the parquet dance floor in front of the stage. "This is for a very special party tonight," said Kohler. "The group has been meeting at Mauna Kea for a hundred years, and every time they come we have to do one better than we did before."

They parked at the end of the Beachfront Wing, and took the shady path along the trickling stream and fishpond, where geckos chirped hello from the flowers and flickering birds answered from higher branches. Behind the tennis courts, they stepped inside the building and walked along the cool terrazzo corridors, past silent, smiling housekeepers with their big carts, and rows of *kapa* tapestries from the South Pacific. "We added these rooms in 1968," said Kohler, "but people still call it the 'new wing.'"

"This is the John Young room," he said, opening the heavy doors. A large sand-colored study of running horses faced the entrance. "He gave us the picture so we named the room after him." Bookshelves lined one wall; a generous sofa faced a widescreen TV. "This is where our guests can watch television," said Kohler, "if they have to."

"That's right. No TVs. Do you get many complaints?"

"No, they love it. We turn on the news every night, here and in the Lloyd Sexton Gallery; show movies a couple times a week, and whatever football game or sports somebody wants to see."

They stopped in the fitness center where Tiffany was earnestly pumping along on a stationery bike. She waved and they kept walking to the swimming pool, then crossed the palm-lined lawn and looped back to pick up the golf cart. Kohler picked up a cocktail napkin and stuffed it into his pocket along with the other bits he'd collected on their tour.

Late in the day, they ended up at the Gazebo Bar at the beach, just before sunset. Out in the bay, the hotel catamaran, Ali'i Kai, was drifting by on her sunset sail.

"Good afternoon, Mr. Meyer," said the bartender.

"Good afternoon, George," said Kohler.

The new Assistant gave them a quizzical look.

"I don't always want the guests to know it's me," said Kohler. "So he calls me Mr. Meyer and I call him George. We've been doing it for years."

"You must be the new Assistant," said the bartender. He served Kohler a white wine with Perrier. "What'll you have? How about a Fredrico?"

"A what?"

"Fredrico. No one has ever died from drinking a Fredrico. After two they're like used cars; they sell themselves. One time I saw somebody drink three. He went to brush something off his shoulder and it was the sidewalk."

"I better have a beer," said the new Assistant.

"Good choice for your first day."

Kohler lifted his glass. "Welcome to the Mauna Kea," he said.

The ocean rumbled in an evening wave. The sun went for a swim and provided a little green flash before turning the sky magenta and turquoise, streaked with gold. Then the sand went silver and the wind cooled, as the beach boys dragged up the last of the chairs and "George" packed up his bar for the night.

They headed up the long stone staircase to meet Chacha for dinner in the Batik. The Restaurant Manager was waiting at the hostess stand with a *lei*. "Good evening, Mr. Scott. This is from the Batik staff." She draped it around his neck and kissed his cheek. "One of the girls made it." She escorted them to Kohler's favorite table by the window where a nice Mondavi Chardonnay was chilling in a silver stand. The Sommelier rushed over with glasses.

"Welcome to Mauna Kea, Mr. Scott," he said, and popped the cork. "I have something very special set aside for your dinner, but this will help you decide what to order." He filled their glasses. Guests waved hello from their tables. A flurry of servers poured water, fluffed napkins, presented menus. With a fair amount of professional theatrics, several courses of elegant dinner were underway.

When Kohler had finished his fish and the other two entrees were still being savored, the Executive Chef rustled out of the kitchen in his long white apron and tall hat.

"Good evening, folks," he said. "How is your dinner?"

"Everything is perfect Chef, thank you," said Kohler. "The *opakapaka* was just a little salty, but nobody would notice that but me. Chacha is enjoying her lamb." She nodded in agreement.

"You must be the new Assistant," said the Chef. He swiped his palm across his apron and reached out to shake hands. "You're having the curry?"

"Outstanding," he said. "I expected to meet a little Thai chef, not a Dutchman."

Chef laughed. "Next time order it with shrimp," he said. "That's the best. I'll go and check on your soufflé."

"We didn't order the soufflé."

"I know; I did," he said as he disappeared back into the kitchen.

The new Assistant had done his best to keep up with Kohler's pace of eating. As soon as the last bite of fish left the plate, he seized the moment and spoke up. "So, Mr. Kohler," he said. "You promised. Where exactly do you come from? And how did you end up in Hawai'i?" Kohler dabbed his mouth with his napkin, and laid it on the tablecloth. He leaned back in his chair.

"I told you I'm a former European," he said. "Actually I am an American Citizen and a Hawaiian at heart. My home country was overtaken by one government after another, and I was always the stranger in town, wherever I ended up in the world." He took a sip of wine. "I was born in Sudetenland, and became a German in 1938. When we were sent to Bavaria, I became a *Rucksack Bayer,* a 'knapsack German,' the same as homeless. When I moved to the northern part of Germany I was a *Verfluchter Bayer,* a Goddamned Bavarian. When I went to Paris, I was a *salle boche,* a filthy German pig. In the U.S., I was a fucking Kraut, excuse me Chacha. In the Virgin Islands, I was 'Whitey;' in Puerto Rico, I was a *gringo,* and here in Hawai'i I'm a *haole.*"

"You certainly seem to have found a home here," said the new Assistant.

"Amen to that," said Kohler. He rationed the last of the wine between their three glasses.

"Here, here," said Chacha. She lifted her glass to chime with theirs. A full bottle thrust into the ice, in place of the empty.

"I think I'd like to hear more," said the new Assistant.

"Somehow, I knew that was coming," said Chacha, placing her fork across her plate. "Well, I've heard the story before. So why don't you two enjoy your soufflé out on the terrace and I'll see you, Adi, back at home?"

"That sounds like a marvelous idea," said Kohler. The gentlemen stood and she gave Kohler a kiss on the cheek, then excused herself for the evening.

As they moved toward the Batik Terrace, dessert forks and fresh napkins appeared like magic at the table outside. The Restaurant Manager followed with the wine, placed the stand and filled their glasses. "Your soufflé will be another few minutes, gentlemen. Would you like us to bring coffee with that?" she asked. "Perhaps brandy and a nice cigar?" Kohler smiled, but shook his head, no.

"In a little while," said the new Assistant. "That would be nice."

The moon was just reaching over the building. In the background, from the lounge, drifted soft strains of smooth jazz and the tinkling of glasses.

"So," said Kohler, "where should I start?"

"How about the beginning?"

Adolf Walter Köhler and Mutti, 1937

CHAPTER 1

This Is What Happened

The world was whirling around on itself, throwing history in every direction. People were trying to make sense of it all and give order to the days. On the day they named December 20, 1936, I was thrown out into this world. My mother called it a *Goldener Sonntag,* a Golden Sunday, the Sunday before Christmas. And she told me that meant I would have a lot of luck in my life.

I learned early on never to argue with Mutti. And if her words were not prophetic, they at least gave me a positive attitude to approach life with, as I struggled to grow older in a changing world that seemed determined I should not.

The country at the moment was named Sudetenland, and most people spoke a language called German. Other people in our country spoke Czech, Russian, some Polish. At the time, we were citizens of the Austrian Ungarian Kingdom. I don't remember much else about the state of the world. It would be many years before I learned the events that led up to the particular moment where I was tangled in history.

What I remember were the changes.

I was almost two years old in the fall of 1938, and I walked with my mother down the streets of Mährisch-Schönberg. We must have been shopping for dinner. Mutti was a wonderful cook and took particular care in selecting the best ingredients for our meals. She let me watch her work in the kitchen of our little house by the park, happily chatting or humming some tune from her own childhood. And sometimes I would lick the big spoon and tell her that the sauce was *sehr gut,* perfect.

People were passing by, saying "Good morning, Frau Köhler." She greeted them, but she was nervous and kept moving without stopping to chat. We had not yet reached the park, and the street was getting very crowded. She held my hand tightly, so tightly it almost hurt my fingers. She looked from side to side at the people around us as she hurried me along. I was very small and struggled to keep up, taking twice as many steps as she did and juggling the loaf of bread she let me carry. I complained I wanted to stop for a candy but she pulled me on.

Her rushing and scolding me were scarier than the crowd, and I was quiet and did as I was told. At the corner we had to stop and there were even more people all lined up along the street. A policeman, tall and powerful looking in his uniform, blew a whistle and held everyone back with a white-gloved hand much bigger even than my father's. I looked at the silver whistle on the silver chain and tried to tell Mutti to look too.

"Hush," she said, "we have to get home." She tried to slip us through the crowd to go around the corner and down the street a different way, but it was no use.

Then I heard a sound that set the hairs on the back of my neck going straight up. Thunder. I looked up through legs and shoulders to what I could see of blue sky straight overhead and didn't understand the sound I heard. Thunder that didn't roll off and die after lightning crackled, but came closer, steadily, rumbling and pounding like my pounding heart.

Mutti pushed me in front of her, till my toes were hanging off the curbstone and I could see the street. All the people's heads were turned in the same direction, watching up the street, where the thunder was coming from, louder now.

Then we saw them. And the mob of people all seemed to take a breath at the same time, then burst into applause and cheers as the soldiers came down the street. All I saw at first was their feet. They were kicking their feet up high and waving one straight arm in time to their marching. And if the policeman's uniform was impressive, theirs were absolutely glorious. Their black boots shone like the marble floor at the church, and their silver buttons glistened like the silver whistle. The soldiers all moved together like one thing, one long centipede of flying hands and boots.

And as the rhythm grew even louder, my own two feet would not keep still, and pattered along on the edge of the curbstone. When they paraded by us, so close you could almost touch them, the solider in the front shouted an order and every one of them snapped his head to the right at once and looked, it seemed, right at me. It took my breath away.

Behind them came trucks and cars with little flags flying, red and white with their *Hackenkreuz* flags, the broken X fluttering. Some of the people on the street had those flags too and I wanted one and I tried to tell my mother so, but she locked me up against her knees and made me be still. She was telling me something, but I couldn't hear what she said, because now the crowd was shouting words, and an even bigger car without a roof was coming down the street.

A man was standing up in the car, a funny-looking little man with a black moustache not nearly as nice as the policeman's. He had on a uniform too, and he raised his arm like the soldiers did, and when he did the crowd screamed out as one voice all together. And I raised my arm and shouted too.

"Heil Hitler! Heil Hitler!"

When we got home Mutti told me she was going to call me Dolfi from now on. Because that was a much nicer name than Adolf for a nice little boy like me.

That was the first change I remember.

Note: The Sudetenland was a region of Bohemian borderlands in the Sudeten mountain range dividing the Republic of Czechoslovakia and Poland. It had been home to predominately German-speaking people for centuries. In the summer of 1938, then-Chancellor Adolf Hitler demanded the union of that area with the Fatherland.

British Prime Minister Neville Chamberlain tried to intervene with diplomacy, but Hitler sent an ultimatum that the problem had to be solved by midnight September 28, and mobilized his infantry and armored troops. At Chamberlain's insistence Hitler delayed his invasion forty-eight hours and arranged a negotiating conference in Munich. He invited Chamberlain, Italy's Benito Mussolini and French Prime Minister Edouard Daladier. Czech President Eduard Bene was not included. The conference became an exercise in "appeasement," resulting in the Munich Pact which permitted German occupation of the Sudetenland. Between October 1st and 10th 1938, history records that Hitler drove through the village of Mährisch-Schönberg.

"Dolfi" and brother Gunter

CHAPTER 2

Nazis

By 1939, the changes spun around me so fast it was impossible to keep up. I heard my mother and father talking about a horrible thing called a war one evening over their coffee. The next evening, it seemed, my mother was having her coffee alone, and my father's plate was absent from the dinner table.

She explained to me that Vati was a soldier now, fighting for the German army far away on the Russian front. I was excited to think of my father marching and kicking his feet up high along the streets in Russia. She told me too that our country was not Sudetenland any- more. It had a new name, like I did. It was Germany now.

My mother and I passed our time together without my father, her calling me the man of the house, and me believing I had a great re- sponsibility to make my father proud. She would cry sometimes at night and I would pretend I didn't hear her, understanding somehow that we were playing at being brave for each other. And just about the time I was getting used to this arrangement, with the two plates on the table, things began to change again. And just as I was getting used to having smaller dinners, and not always having milk enough for a second glass, I noticed my mother was getting fat.

This astonished me, and her explanations to her very curious son made no sense to me. But nothing prepared me for the astonishment of having my brother Gunter arrive, on June 7, 1939. Now my re- sponsibilities as man of the house, at age two and a half, had doubled. I decided enough was enough.

"When is my Vati coming home?" I asked.

"Soon," was all she said.

I watched the baby growing every day and listened to him cry. I tried to explain to him sometimes how we were not supposed to cry all the time, but rather be good soldiers and so forth. I couldn't make him understand any more than Mutti could make me understand why the baby got the milk and I drank tea with my dinner as she did.

People came to talk to my mother one day. They left her with some papers to read and said they would be back. I asked her to read them to me and she said they were nothing. When the people came back they were mean to her and she raised her voice to them. It made the baby cry. She told me to sit with him and make him stop, and she closed the bedroom door to talk to those people.

I made faces at Gunter until he laughed and forgot about his crying. I could hear my mother talking in the other room. She told them her husband was away from home, that he was a soldier in the German army and she refused to be in their party. I didn't understand this at all. Why wouldn't Mutti want to go to a party? I wanted to go to a party.

Finally I heard the front door close. My mother came in to pick up Gunter. She thanked me for being good to him.

"Who were those people?" I asked.

"They are Nazis," she said.

"What's a Nazi?"

"That is a person who belongs to a political party, and who wants everybody else to belong too."

"What party is that?"

"It's a government party," she said. "It's not a party for fun."

It wasn't long after that that Mutti began doing more strange things. She was cleaning out closets and cupboards and giving our things away to our neighbors. I couldn't believe this.

"Why?" was my constant question, seldom answered.

"Because we don't need them anymore," said my mother.

"We have to ask Vati," I insisted.

"Vati won't mind," she said. "He will understand."

This was all acceptable for a while, until it came to the matter of toys. I didn't have many playthings, as most children in those days, but those I did have were precious to me. I don't even remember the toy car or stick horse or rag doll she was trying to get rid of, but I had to put my small foot down.

"No," I said. "That is mine."

"Yes," said Mutti, "it used to be your toy when you were little. But you are a big boy now."

"I am?"

"Of course you are," said Mutti, "and when we reach our new home, you will find things to play with like the other big boys."

New home? This was another change I was unprepared for.

"What new home?"

"Our new *wohnung,* an apartment on the edge of the city, right on the very city wall. It is a smaller house, and we will not have room for all these things."

"But why are we going to a new apartment?"

"Because it will be safer for us to live there."

"What about Vati? Does he know we are moving?"

"Yes."

"How? How will he find us?"

"I have written a letter to him. He will be able to find us when he comes home."

"When is he coming home?"

"I don't know, Dolfi," she said, "but he will come home."

"What will happen to our house?"

"The Nazi Chief will move into it."

"Why?"

My mother looked at me with her knowing eyes, and gave me a little hug. She was very tired, and I knew she would soon be tired of my questions and tell me to hush or go play. I had to make every one count. I asked her again, mid-hug, "Why?"

"Because the Nazi's need our house for some people in their party," she said, "and so we have to move out. The Nazi people will live here and we will live in our new apartment on the edge of the city."

"Why? Why can't they live in their own house?"

"It is their house now," she said. "Now go and see about your brother."

"But…"

"Hush now," she said. "Go and play."

I left her to her packing, and went to explain to my brother. This I assumed as part of my new responsibility as a Big Boy and the man of the house. It was not going to be easy for him to understand, but I would help. And I would help my mother too. But I knew my father was not going to like this. He was not going to be happy when he got home and found a Nazi party going on with strange people in his house. Oh, he was not going to like that at all.

I couldn't wait.

Dolfi at his First Communion (back row, third from the left)

CHAPTER 3

Shelling

As the days went by and the war talk grew as common as the weather talk, everything started to change. Even Mutti looked different. She was always watching everything, and her eyes flickered around all the time. Her head turned when she walked, back-and-forth, watching. She watched us, everything we did, like she might miss something, like we might have a secret. She was so careful about everything, careful about the bread and the milk, careful about counting Deutsche Marks and putting them back in her purse. Careful to speak quietly, careful whom she talked to. She didn't smile very much anymore. In the evenings she sat with the neighbors and listened to the radio for news. We were not allowed to make a sound.

I didn't understand this change and I didn't understand who had replaced my happy mother with this sad one. It was not fair.

But there wasn't time to dwell on such things, not with a new home and a new neighborhood to explore, not to mention a new baby brother, and everywhere excitement and whispers among the adults. They all seemed as busy and distracted as Mutti, which was lucky for us because they ignored us, except for the old people. The old people were moving slower, spending a lot more time on the benches in the park. They were there every day, men and women, sitting and watching everything go on around us, like they didn't want to miss anything right now. They looked at me and smiled, very nice smiles, like I had done something nice for them, or like somebody taking a walk on the last day of fall, when they know it's going to snow that night. Old people knew things like that.

Church had changed too. It was crowded. The Mass was endless. The whole town, it looked like, lined up and slowly, slowly wound to the altar rail to hear the priest say, *"in nominum Corpus Christo, in nominum Corpus Christo."* He had to say it so many times that he looked very tired by the time I got up to him with Mutti. Sometimes his hand would shake when he put the wafer on her tongue. It took forever, and after church the adults stood together in little groups talking to each other importantly and turning their heads back-and-forth like my mother did.

The children did what children do. We played. We played war, of course, dividing up into imaginary armies and killing each other with sticks. We stomped up and down the sidewalks, goose-stepping, saluting each other and saying "Heil Hitler." It made some people laugh. The baker's wife was one who did not laugh. If she saw us while she was sweeping the walk in front of her shop, she would shake the broom at us and tell us to go home. We would run and continue our little war elsewhere.

I missed Vati terribly. He was not an easy father. He was strict, of course, as all fathers were in those days. And a lot of fathers had gone away to be soldiers, but they were all coming back. We knew that.

I somehow missed his strictness. He made me work on small jobs around the house, and he made us speak properly and dress properly and do what we were expected to do. He himself worked very hard, always, and it seemed he never smiled, except to other people when he said good morning or good evening, shaking hands with someone on the street. Then he smiled and looked like he was happy for a minute, then it was time to move on.

With Vati it was always time to move on. It was always time to do something. I used to think he had a schedule for everything, including when to sneeze and when to go to the bathroom. Dinner was served, when he was home, exactly at the same time every evening, and there was always bread. We always ate everything we were given, and we never asked for more unless it was offered.

After dinner, he and Mutti talked at the table for a time and we were expected to be quiet. If we had finished eating, we were allowed to carry our plates into the kitchen and then play quietly. I ate very fast so I could leave the table fast. I was bored by grownup conversation, all business and schedules and what we did and what we were going to do and nothing fun. And the war of course.

It was like the smiling. The only time there were stories told or any fun at the table, was when other grownups came to dinner. Then Mutti would cook something wonderful, *Kartoffel* (potatoes) and *sauerkraut mit sauerbraten* (cabbage and marinated beef) or *schweine goulasch* (pork stew). Vati would open bottles of beer and they would laugh and even sometimes sing and I would want to be just like him at that moment. I wanted to be a man who could make people happy and comfortable in my house. I loved to watch them clink their glasses together and say "Prost" and take a sip.

I loved to watch him tell a story and make everyone laugh. Especially Mutti. After the guests left, Vati would wash the beer glasses and dry them and put them away in the cabinet, like he put his smile away until the next time company would come.

Now there wasn't any company of course. And there wasn't any Vati. My mother didn't work, so he must have sent her money and that must have been one reason she was so careful with the Deutsche Marks in her purse and the slices of bread. I don't know how she managed, but it never occurred to me to doubt for a moment that she could.

Unlike my father, Mutti was a living smile. She had a way of looking at you that made you think she knew exactly what you'd been up to, good or bad. This might be a look that all mothers have, and it might be a trick, just to get you to confess whatever you'd broken or hidden or done to your little brother when nobody was looking. More than that though, she would look at me and know when the tears over a skinned knee or a smashed thumb were generated from real hurt, or just an excuse to get a hug. She always hugged me anyway. She seemed to understand what I really wanted, no matter how I was acting. It's hard to explain, but it's something I always admired about her.

But all that was before. That was normal life. Now it was just us and Mutti and we did the best we could.

One night after dinner, after a story, after we were in bed, my mother came into the room and shook me awake, hard, with a scared voice. "Wake up Dolfi. Help me with your brother. Wake up now Liebchen, we have to go to church."

Church? This made no sense to me. It wasn't Christmas. There was no midnight Mass. It could not possibly be Sunday morning. I knew nothing, but only felt a danger in the air and jumped out of bed. Mutti was grabbing up my baby brother. I got dressed in a hurry and tried to help her find his things. She was in such a rush, like Vati. Time to go. Now.

There was a sound coming from overhead, a horrible sound. Whistling, a shrieking monster whistle, and explosions. Terrible bangs and crashes and explosions somewhere outside. As Mutti wrapped a blanket around my brother, a huge bang rattled the windows in our apartment. I heard breaking glass in the street.

She stopped fussing and we rushed out of the apartment. She locked the door and put the key in her pocket. There were a lot of people on the street and all of them ran in the same direction, toward the church. The street was full of dust and smoke and noise. I could hear the fire trucks and sirens not too far away.

Boom, another explosion followed by screams and sounds of panic.

"Run Dolfi," said my mother. "Hurry, stay close to me."

I grabbed for her hand in the dark, but she was holding my brother so I took a corner of her skirt and we ran down our street toward the church. I thought I must be dreaming. Even the street didn't feel normal anymore. Even the sound of our feet on the pavement sounded wrong, felt wrong.

We passed a couple of houses then Mutti ran up to one of the neighbor's doors. She didn't even knock, just ran inside.

"But this is not the church," I said.

"Hush," she said, "come inside now."

We went in and through the Schwartz's living room and to the top of their cellar steps. I couldn't believe my mother was doing something so rude. My father would never have done such a crazy thing.

But I never let go of her skirt. Hans Peter Schwartz had told me there were ghosts in his house's cellar, and even though I had been dying to go down and see them all this time, now I was terrified. Maybe the ghosts had got out, escaped into our city and were shrieking through the sky and blowing up the buildings.

"No," I told my mother. "We can't go down there."

"Come at once," she said, "do as I say."

"I'm afraid to go down there," I said. I stood on the top step, holding her skirt.

"Come anyway," she said. "Now."

"No," I said. "We can't. There are ghosts in the cellar."

"This is not a ghost, Dolfi," she said. "This is a war."

War. I went with her and said nothing else. This was what a war sounded like.

There were other people in the cellar, and there was a light. They pointed directions and we went through another door which lead into another basement of the house next to the Schwartz's. I could hear rushing feet and clipped voices ahead. I could see a little light. We crossed from one basement to the next to the next, all along the block, all the while under the shrieks and bombardment of the war ghost. I kept thinking, war is real. It is not just conversation and games in the park. This is war and it's real.

It was like learning the Devil was real.

Finally we reached the basement that belonged to the church. Everyone was there, but there was no Mass. The Priest was in a chair in the back, reading the Bible in German instead of Latin. People were very quiet but he read loudly in his old voice, and he could be heard over the explosions and the crying and the whispered, unanswered questions in the room.

I thought about Vati. I wondered if this was what a real war sounded like every day and if this was what his life was like: the horrible noises, the horrible fear. I thought it wasn't fair that he should not be with us, thought how much we needed him, and I wondered if he was afraid. The thought of Vati afraid made me very afraid.

It was the longest night of my short life. I had never been so scared or seen my mother so scared. I was jealous of my brother, blissfully sleeping in her lap. I wanted to wake him up but that would make him cry and that would make me cry. I watched him and I waited.

We didn't know when the sun came up. We stayed in there, listening to the Bible and watching the rosaries roll over the fingers of the nuns. Finally the spaces grew longer between the explosions, then finally the shrieking and the bombing stopped. The Father Priest went up to see what was happening outside.

He came back and said it was safe, and we left, slowly, in little clumps of people walking back to our houses. Some people's houses were gone. I had forgotten about the ghost, but now I hoped he had been killed by the war.

Our apartment was still there. My mother got the key out of her pocket and unlocked the door. We went inside and she gave us a bath and something to eat. The milk was spoiled so we drank tea. My mother opened my father's bottle of brandy and had a little drink. Her hands stopped shaking. It was dark outside, as it had been when we left. I watched her sit at the kitchen table beside my father's empty chair and I knew, as she knew for me so many times. I could not think what she was thinking in her grownup mind full of worries and other things, but I knew, so I put my arms around her neck and pressed my cheek against her hair.

"It will be all right, Mutti," I said.

I thought she was crying but there were no tears in her eyes. I thought she might have run out of tears.

"Yes it will," she said. "But not for a long, long time."

Mutti and her sons

CHAPTER 4

Little Horses

In 1941 I started going to school, but this, finally, was a change I was prepared for, had been waiting for in fact, for a long time. In spite of the war, I was anxious to get on with the business of growing up. I was five years old and Gunter, at age two, was sufficiently grown, at least in my opinion, to take on the man-of-the-house business during the day.

I could read a little bit already, had read Gunter some stories, and made up the parts when I didn't know the words. He didn't seem to mind, particularly if whatever I said made him laugh.

I liked walking to school. It was only ten or fifteen minutes from our house by the city wall, but to me it was an adventure every day as I struck out with my knapsack full of books. I learned my ABC's and numbers quickly and worked hard to always make good grades. This was important to me from the very beginning. I wanted to learn everything I needed to know, I wanted to excel, and I wanted my mother to be proud of me. When I got my report card, or a good grade on an *aufsatz* (essay), I brought the papers home to Mutti as seriously as my father had brought his pay into the house, and nothing pleased me more than hearing her say that they were good.

We studied German as our "official" language, along with spelling, math, history, *Erdkunde* (world events), all taught by lay teachers. Religious classes were taught by priests. In the beginning, there wasn't much difference between the ABC's and the Hail Mary's. I listened to what the priests said in class, and to what they said in Latin at the Mass, although I didn't understand those words at all.

I watched every move of the altar boys in their long robes and wondered how they could remember all the proper things to do at the proper time. It was very impressive. I started to sing in the boy's choir, much to Mutti's delight, and soon became a fair soprano, for a while. I loved to stand in front of the church and sing, and to watch Mutti smiling at me, especially if she was supposed to have her head bowed.

I even spent some time training to be an altar boy. I helped the priests with their fancy vestments and watched them drink perhaps a bit more of the consecrated wine than was absolutely necessary for religious purposes.

I grew a little bigger and learned to do new things each year in school. Gunter grew too, and I was able to talk with him in regular conversations now, trying to teach him to write his name or draw a horse or otherwise make himself useful. My mother continued to keep house and cook meals and do whatever it is mothers do that had nothing to do with their children, even though we could not imagine such a thing. Life had at least a feeling of normality.

One time we were invited to a family reunion in Schönau. All the relatives would be there, if we could come. Mutti counted all her Deutsche Marks and decided we should go. We would make the trip by train. I was very excited and couldn't wait for the day to come. I packed my own things and got ready very early that day, looking at the clock every five minutes until it was time to go. Mutti wasn't ready. I tried to help but all I managed to do was annoy her and make Gunter cry.

Then, on the way to the station she stopped for something at a shop and we were delayed even more. I couldn't believe it. Vati would never have allowed this. When it was time to go, it was time to go. If I was the man of the house now, then it was my job to get us to the train on time. My hands balled up into fists and I paced up and down in front of the store front. My face felt red-hot. When she finally came out, I grabbed her hand and tugged her down the street.

We reached the station in time to see the train just pulling out. It puffed steam and rumbled away. I had to scream to be heard over the racket.

"We missed the train!"

"I'm sorry, Dolfi," said my mother.

"We missed the train and it's your fault! Vati never would have made us late!"

"Hush, Dolfi. Calm down," she said. "We'll just have to take the next one."

"It's your fault!" I said. "You're always late! It's your fault! It's your fault!"

She just looked at me. I couldn't stop my tantrum till it ran its course, and when it did I was sweaty and out of breath. I had lost my temper. I had lost my temper with my mother. We were both amazed. I felt something had changed inside of me, but I didn't know what it was. All I knew for sure was that I would never, ever miss another train as long as I lived. I watched the engine shrink away down the track.

We eventually made what turned out to be an uneventful trip, boring for me, visiting relatives I'd never met and would probably never see again. We kept hearing different versions of the same bad news from family in other parts of the country. There was a war. People were frightened. There was much serious talk and much listening to the radio. Most of it stopped if we children came anywhere within hearing. I thought there was more crying than necessary when it was time to go home.

After we got back, Vati must have visited. But those memories are not as clear as his long, long absences, occasional letters my mother read to us at the kitchen table, and his photograph on the wall always admonishing us to be good. We tried.

It was never clear, in the fragments of conversations or the radio speeches we did hear, who the enemy was. We heard a lot about Hitler and terrible things happening in Germany and Poland, but we didn't know what was true and what was made up to frighten us. I never really knew who was fighting together and who was fighting against each other: the Germans and Russians, the Russians and

Czechs. I heard stories about the Italians, the English, the French and after December, the Americans, but none of it meant very much to me. To me the enemy was the war itself, looming just outside the city walls, ready to screech into our city at any moment, like the ghost from the Schwartz's basement.

In the spring of 1944 it did.

There was a long tunnel from the city walls leading into our town. The mouth of the tunnel opened up onto a street that led into the center of town, where the marketplace was. The marketplace was surrounded by businesses and buildings, which were in turn surrounded by people's houses and churches. Around everything was the city wall. So far, even with the shelling and the awareness of a constant threat, the wall made us feel relatively safe. It was the fall of the year and I was almost eight years old, in the middle of the third grade.

One day, Mutti and Gunter and I were at the market, doing what shopping we had money for. I kept Gunter occupied while my mother looked at a few potatoes in one of the stalls. I heard a sound I had never heard before, a strange rumbling, echoing and growing from the direction of the tunnel. I thought instantly it must be collapsing and I ran for my mother. She put the potatoes back down into the stand, as everyone turned to listen to this rumbling, and now shouting. I thought it must be people dying in the caved-in tunnel. Except that it was growing closer.

Some of the people started running. My mother grabbed us, one in each hand, somehow the curiosity pulling us harder than the fear was holding us back, and we ran immediately toward the tunnel with everyone else. I was very excited, too excited to even ask questions, as the noise grew louder and louder. The rumble was starting to sound familiar, like something I'd heard before.

Horses, a lot of horses. Riders whooping and screaming and firing rifles into the air. The gunshots and the horses' hoofs pounded and echoed off the walls of the tunnel. We couldn't see them yet, but they were coming towards us, and they were coming fast.

Then breaking glass and frightened screams added to the mix of crashes and smashes, neighing horses and barking dogs. Church bells clanged and sirens started to wail. People turned and ran back to their homes and away from the war riding into our town.

Then we saw them. Thundering, screaming, animal-men. Ugly dark men in furs and rags, kicking ugly little shaggy horses, foaming and steam-breathed, huffing and rumbling down the street, over bicycles and flower pots and anything in their way.

"It's the Mongols!" someone said. "The Russians have won the war!"

Russians. These were the enemy. And they had won. And they were here to kill us all.

We ran. Everyone ran. In the marketplace, chaos began that would last for days, as these Mongols began their rampage by shooting the vendors who did not run, and stealing what the dead left behind. They stole the bread. They stole the fruit and the beer. They stole the potatoes that my mother had put back in the stall. And when it all was stolen, they destroyed the shops and fought among themselves.

We barricaded ourselves inside the apartment and waited. The sounds of destruction, the shouts of victory in a language we could not understand continued. I hoped they would kill each other off and we could find their dead bodies in the marketplace in the morning.

Later in the day, the neighbors knocked on the door and shared what news there was, and what food there was. Frau Kowatch and her husband had heard terrible things were happening in the center of town, so terrible they and my mother didn't bother to whisper while I sat there. Herr Kowatch had his pistol in his hand.

"They have taken over the police station," said Herr Kowatch. "They are taking men from their houses, and lining them up in the streets."

"That can't be true," said my mother. "Where are the Germans? Where are Hitler's troops?"

I thought about my father. He was with Hitler.

"What about the Nazis?" asked Mutti. "Are they killing them too?"

"I don't know," said Herr Kowatch. "Nobody knows."

"They are hurting everyone!" said Mrs. Kowatch. "They are destroying everything." She started to cry.

"Hush," said her husband. He turned to my mother and spoke softly. "They are," he said, "raping the women and dragging the young girls away."

I knew what that was. I knew where babies came from. I knew what a sin sex was with a woman who was not your wife. And I knew that forcing a woman to do that was a bigger sin still. Big as murder.

A rider appeared on the corner, then several more. Herr Kowatch took his wife's hand and pulled her back toward their house. "There is nothing we can do," he said. "Don't fight them. Think of the children." The riders approached.

"Go inside, boys," my mother said, and took a deep breath.

I looked at my mother, whose gentle eyes had frozen into hardened determination, and I was ready to sin to protect her. I was ready somehow, with the kitchen knife or the fireplace poker, to kill a Russian and go to hell on the spot.

"No," I told her.

They came closer. They were not screaming and shooting as the other Mongols had done. They did not have to. They had us. They stopped their horses and walked up to us, arrogant, not even in a hurry. We stood in our doorway and watched them come.

One of them was taller and his clothes were different. He looked like an officer, in charge of the others. His skin was lighter, and I thought he must be what they call a "White Russian," and the others were "Black Russians" because they were so dark. This man told my mother to go inside, then he turned to Gunter and me.

"March into the house," he said. "Go into your room and stay there. I do not want to see you when I come in."

"No," I told him and kicked his shin as hard as I could. He grabbed me and said something I didn't understand. I punched my small fist into his stomach but it had no impact. He dragged us into the kitchen and locked the door.

I sat with my back to the door, unable to move. I stared at the kitchen walls, and they didn't look like they belonged to our kitchen any more. I didn't think I could stand. I didn't think I could breathe unless I concentrated. And I did. And for a while the only thing I could hear was the loud pound of my own heartbeat.

In a while, if I concentrated hard enough, I could hear my mother's voice. She was talking calmly but I couldn't quite hear all the words. She was pleading with him, and she might have been crying, but she sounded somehow strong and I was very very proud of her. It strengthened my own small resolve.

I could hear the Russians grunting and complaining and banging around in our house and I thought I heard the front door open and close as some of them went outside to wait. I could hear what I assumed was the one officer talking back to my mother, in German. Some of the words were German. No and yes and Fräulein and something else. They must have gone into the bedroom. I heard the horses whuffing and stomping outside and the filthy Mongols garbling among themselves. Gunter had cried himself to sleep on the floor.

The kitchen door opened and I jumped up with all the courage I could muster. I would face down this monster like a man.

It was the officer, and he just stood there looking at me. My mother was behind him. She did not look raped. She did not look harmed at all. The officer said something in his strange accent, something about he was sorry to disturb us. Then he left. I could not believe it.

Later I learned he was a doctor, and Mutti with her calm and continuous questioning, had found he knew a little bit of German. She talked to him, not even knowing what he understood. She told him she was having her monthly and with some verification of this fact I guess embarrassment scared away his need. And so he left, and his men were laughing and he told them something which must have meant shut up because they rode very quietly after that. I could hear the hoofbeats for a long way up the road. Even over my sobbing and my mother's. Even over the horror that had come to our town and the horror that was on its way.

The riot continued for days, but eventually the Mongols went away, leaving their destruction and their dead. There was only a little relief in seeing them go, for we did not know what might come next. Are we Russians now? I thought to myself. Not Germans, not Czechs, not

Bohemians. Russians! The same as the ugly men and their ugly little horses. What could be worse?

If we knew the future, I think we would invent a way to hold onto the present for dear life. If we'd had any idea of the things that were still ahead of us, we might have chosen the rioting Mongols. But I did know one thing that shined a little ray of hope through the long dark tunnel of our town. The war was over, whoever had won.

And that meant Vati would come home.

Note: In November, 1938 Czechoslovakia was divided into three autonomous units: Slovakia, Ruthenia and Bohemia/Moravia, which included the former Sudetenland. By March 1939, Hitler had control of the Czech government, and forced Bohemia/Moravia to become a German protectorate. Although they had been allies since the beginning of the war, Germany turned and attacked the Soviet Union on June 22, 1941. After years of bitter fighting, Russian troops began to re-take their occupied lands. In April 1944, supported by American forces and a Czech coalition government headed by former president Eduard Bene, the Soviets drove into Bohemia/Moravia.

Vati as a soldier

In the field

CHAPTER 5

Stranger

Four days after the end of the war there were only two men in the entire town, and they were the priests. The women started the work of putting food back on the tables, and a semblance of reason back into life, one day at a time. The schools were closed to students and turned into hospitals. We children had nothing to do but try and help with the work. Strangers who passed through what was left of our village were treated as well as we could treat them. We exchanged a little food for news, and we sent them on their way to wherever they were going.

One day another unknown man came limping down our street with a stick. I hoped he wouldn't stop and bother us; I couldn't help it. He was very skinny, and filthy, and his beard was long and scraggly. He looked like a goblin from a fairy tale and I didn't want him to talk to me. I looked down at my shoes and pretended he wasn't there, but he waved his hand at me and kept coming closer.

"Dolfi," he said. "Look at you."

"How do you know my name?" I stared at him.

"You're such a big boy now," he said. "Practically all grown up."

I wanted him to go away.

"Don't you remember me?" he asked. "Look here, don't you know who I am?"

I didn't know, and I didn't care.

"Come a little closer, now. Let me get a look at you, at least." He took a step.

My mother opened the front door and caught her breath. And something in the way he looked at her, and something I felt fly over my head between them was more than familiar. I looked at this ragged stranger opening his arms for my mother. And I knew. And I stayed put, and let them crush me between them. My father was home. My father was home. My father was home.

Vati had been shot in the ankle, which probably saved his life. He was released from the hospital two or three weeks before the end of the war. When it was over, the general told his men they were on their own. About a hundred kilometers from home, the first thing my father did was find a farm. He knocked on the door, and begged the family there to help him with some civilian clothes. He traded his uniform and what money he had for the farmer's old pants and shirts and socks. Then he started walking home.

Now I was confident everything would begin to go back to the way it used to be. That's what I thought. But one has to be a lot older to learn just how wrong he can be.

There was no food to buy. There was no work. There was nothing to be done. And as the other fathers came home, or didn't come home, there was news. Things were very bad, much worse in some places than here.

We were fortunate that my father spoke a little Russian, and somehow became the chauffeur for the Russian Town Commandant. He worked very hard and very long hours for no money, but he was given one suit of clothes and he got to bring home food every night.

My mother did what she could. Some of the farms had leftover produce that the Mongols didn't take. We learned to find mushrooms in the woods and other things. We learned to share, and to trade. Mutti kept telling us not to grow so fast, so we could keep wearing our clothes and our shoes. My shoes were always too tight and I complained every time I had to put them on. But bigger shoes required two pairs of socks, and that was out of the question.

It was fall, and Mutti worried about the winter. So did everybody. But winter doesn't care if you worry or not. Winter comes anyway. The war was over; another change had come.

CHAPTER 6

The Sawmill

Our family and our town and what was left of our country was no longer Russia, no longer Germany, no longer Sudetenland. Now it was 1946; we were part of Communist Czechoslovakia; our town was now called "Cumpberc" instead of Mährisch-Schönberg and we were supposed to speak Czech instead of German. I was beginning to think it didn't make any difference what country you belonged to, that governments shifted back-and-forth across borders of countries the way the wind blew at the change of seasons. And governments didn't care about the people living in those countries any more than the wind did.

The beautiful parks, the streets, the public buildings which were ruined by the war, were all left to be rubble. There were no more street cleaners or gardeners early in the mornings. The Communists, at least as far as I could see, had no interest in making the ugliness go away, or in making things at all the way they used to be.

Our old house by the park did survive. On the rare occasions when Vati would take me sledding, I would look at the front door wistfully as we walked by. Then we would trek on up the hill for the pure cold thrill of racing down, to climb back up and do it over again. It was one of the few things that made winter tolerable.

There had been a sawmill in our town. The father of my friend Günter Jellinek owned it. In the days before the war, farmers would bring their cut trees to the mill in horse-drawn wagons. The millers trimmed them down into lumber, and the farmers carried back the brand new boards.

The sawmill closed when the fighting started. Our school was still a hospital, so our days were left to our own amusement. One day Günter Jellinek and I, and some of the other boys, played at the saw-mill in the afternoon. We explored the empty offices and rusted ma-chinery the way deep-sea divers might a shipwreck. The older boys would go there too, to smoke cigarettes made from cornsilks when they couldn't find tobacco, and pass around some food or a bottle of homemade schnapps they might have stolen. The older boys never talked to us, of course, and if we came too close they told us to go away.

We also made a game of finding things to eat. The whole town did this. In the fall, after the potato fields were harvested, we could go and pick up what was left. Günter Jellinek and I intended to go frog-gigging down at the pond. We had our sharpened sticks and a bucket, and a big bet going on who was going to catch the one with the fattest legs.

On the way, we saw the big boys leaving the potato field, and followed them, as much by smell as by sight because they had a fire going at the old sawmill and were cooking potatoes to eat.

"Can we have some?" I asked, brave because I was hungry.

"Go away," they said.

"Please," I tried again. "We'll bring you some more wood for your fire."

They ignored us.

"Look here," said Günter, "this is my father's sawmill, and if you're going to use it, you have to share."

One of the boys, a real bully named Krubuchek, picked up a stone. "Go away, *Arschloch*," he said, and threatened to throw it.

"Come on, Günter," I said and tugged him by the arm. "Let's go."

We walked back through the potato patch on our way to the frog pond, arguing about what we might do to bullies like that when we were big enough. We made fun of the one who threatened us with the rock, and kicked the dust and practiced using the bad words we knew. Günter noticed there were still potatoes in the ground. We stopped to pick up some of them and thought we would show them, we'd make our own fire and have our own potato feast.

We gathered up kindling and potatoes; only the smallest, hardest ones were left, and ran back to the sawmill. We picked a spot outside the compound so the big boys wouldn't see us, and found a piece of steel for an oven plate. In a while, we had a decent fire. We cooked and ate our potatoes, and relished every bite, kissing our fingers like the French chefs do. We were extremely proud of our oven and our meal and our secret success.

When we were finished, we put the fire out and buried the ashes, stamping it carefully as we had been taught. We hid the oven plate so the big boys wouldn't steal it, and went off on our frog hunt. We were fairly successful with that too, and pretty soon the bucket was full enough to where the frogs could almost jump out, but we were tied at three frogs apiece. One more, and then we'd go home. The loser would have to carry the bucket back.

Günter noticed something. "Look at that," he said.

I stopped stalking a particularly fat one. There was smoke in the sky, a long dark cloud pointing one accusing black finger down at the sawmill.

"It's a fire," I said. "Let's go!"

We left our bucket and ran toward the smoke as fast as we could. It was the sawmill, and it was surrounded by smoke and flames. People were everywhere. Sirens wailed. A lot of people were watching and trying to help the firemen. The big boys were there too.

"There they are!" They pointed at us, running up.

We froze in our tracks. Günter looked at me with panicked eyes. We were thinking the same thing. We put the fire out. We know we put it out. Some policemen started heading our way. We ran for all we were worth, ducking through the shortcuts that only we knew and cutting through the neighborhoods like a wind.

We both made it home. My mother was out, so I didn't have to answer why I looked so scared and was so out of breath, and what happened to my frog-gig and my bucket. I cleaned myself up and was trying to act normal when she returned, relieved to see me home and safe, after hearing about the big fire at the sawmill.

Later that night, when my brother was asleep and Mutti and I were drinking our tea, there was a knock at the door. Mutti opened it and faced two policemen. My heart didn't stop, but it tried to jump out of my chest to get away. They marched into our house and grabbed me.

"Stop," said my mother. "What is this about? What has he done?"

One of the policemen had a paper. "He and his friend set fire to the Jellinek Mill," he said.

"No Mutti!" I cried. "It's not true! We didn't."

"Wait," said my mother. "Let me see that paper. How do you know this?"

He flagged it in front of her face. I couldn't run. I couldn't do anything. Their hands were clamped to my arms.

"The others said they saw them light the fire. Him and his friend, the Jellinek boy. It is a crime to destroy the property of the provisional government."

"Children," said my mother. "They're children. Not criminals. There must be a mistake. Please wait. Wait until my husband comes home. He is the driver for the Town Commandant."

The two men exchanged a look, as if they didn't believe her. I thought I was going to throw up. My chest was heaving in and out, like sobbing with no tears.

"No mistake, Fräulein," said the policeman. "The Jellinek boy was acting for his father. They purposely destroyed the sawmill to keep it out of the hands of the Czech and Russian officials."

"It's wrong," said my mother. "It's a mistake. Please. Wait."

She looked desperately around the dark street. A few of the neighbors had opened their doors to see what was going on. My mother called their names. She reached for me. "Tell them," she said to me, kissing my face. "Just tell them the truth."

They took me. They took me out of my house and my mother's arms, over her screams and demands and cries for help to the neighbors. Into their car. Down the street. Through the dark night. Past the ruin of our town. Past the point of any hope that I would live to be eleven. They took me to jail.

Günter Jellinek was there. They kept us separated, but we saw each other from time to time. If his face was a mirror of mine, then I looked terrible. I looked like someone who had been frightened to death but didn't know he was dead. My eyes were wide like a shying horse, and my quivering bottom lip would not be still. My fists were clenched and my face was the color of the moon. I nodded at Gunter. There was nothing we could do. Nothing I could think of but my mother's words. Just tell the truth.

The time in jail was a dark blur. They interrogated me. Between the question sessions, I tried to sleep in a black, rancid cell, and had terrible dreams. I could not believe my father did not come to rescue me. They must have fed me something, but I don't remember. I remember being filthy and hungry. I remember being very, very scared.

Once they took me into a small room with only one policeman, a chair and a desk. They stood me in front of the officer at the desk and left me there.

"You set the fire," he said. "You and your friend."

"We didn't do it," I said.

"We know you did. We have witnesses."

"I don't care. We didn't do it."

"You did. Say you did."

"Sir, we did not," I said again. I wished I had counted how many times I said this. I prayed to all the saints I knew that Gunter was saying the same thing.

"You set the fire in the sawmill," said the policeman. "Herr Jellinek told you to do it."

"That's not true," I said.

He opened a drawer in the desk and took out a ruler. I knew what was coming. I thought of the nuns and hard lessons learned in school. I focused on the ruler and it somehow made me feel better. This was something I understood. Let him come, I thought. I'm not afraid of the ruler.

He walked slowly around the desk to where I stood. I watched the ruler in his hand. As he got closer I realized I was wrong. Those hard eyes did not belong to a sister, and this was not a catechism class. I took a deep breath. Here it comes.

He grabbed me and tore down my pants to my knees, bent me over the desk and held my neck while he spanked my naked bottom with the ruler. Every time he beat me I cried out "We didn't do it!" I said it forty-four times, until he was sweating and raging and I was almost crazy with pain.

"We didn't do it," I said. Forty-five.

After two days I stopped worrying about Günter. He was either telling them the same thing I was, and that was why they were so frustrated with us. Or, he was dead already and they had to get the story out of me. It was easier now. I stopped thinking about getting away or convincing them I was innocent. I stopped thinking about my mother. I only thought about my one sentence every time the question was asked and staying alive long enough to say it one more time.

On the evening of the second day they took me back to the little room with the desk. There was a different policeman sitting there, a Czech. He was a mean-faced, dark-haired man with a pushbroom moustache. He told me to sit in the chair. He opened the desk drawer. I didn't understand. If he was going to beat me, why should I sit? But I was long past caring or believing any of this should make sense, so I sat and waited for the ruler.

What came out of the drawer was a revolver.

My jaw dropped. The hair stood up on the back of my neck. I thought I was going to pee in the chair.

The policeman moved slowly. He flicked open the chamber and looked inside where the bullets go. He looked down the barrel, then closed the gun, and with his thumb slid the safety off. He pushed back the chair and stood up. He walked deliberately around the side of the desk, muttering to himself and shaking his head. He approached me on my left and held the gun in front of my eyes. He let me take a long, long look.

"You burned down the sawmill," he said.

This time I couldn't speak my sentence. I stared at the blue steel, at the trigger.

"You burned down the sawmill."

I shook my head.

"Admit it," he said. His thumb clicked the hammer slowly back. "Or I will shoot you."

My voice came back. "Please don't do that," I cried out. "I told you. I told everyone. I told you over and over again and it's the truth. We didn't do it. We didn't do it. Please."

He moved in and pressed the gun to my temple. I could feel the cold little circle on the side of my head. I could hear the bullets talk to me. You're dead, they said.

I whispered, "We didn't do it."

I heard his hand shift, his finger on the trigger, the trigger squeeze in, the bullets whisper.

Click.

Metal hit metal and the gun jerked on my head, but my head did not explode. I opened my clenched eyes and blinked, numb with astonishment at being alive. The Czech policeman was laughing.

On the morning of the third day Mutti was able to get me out of there. My father had been away and so she managed it by herself. I don't know how; I never asked. A couple of days later I saw Günter and we hugged each other. He had done the same thing, repeated the same story over and over, and that may have saved our lives.

Not long after, they took some of our other schoolmates, the bigger boys who had accused us of setting the fire. They kept them for several days, just like us. One of them, the one named Krubuchek, was beaten so badly he ended up in the hospital and died.

Later, we heard that a man who worked for Herr Jellinek many years was angry at losing his job to the war. When he saw us playing at cooking our potatoes, he got the idea for the arson. He lit the fire for revenge and disappeared.

I thought about revenge for a long, long time when I heard that story. I thought about the sawmill where nobody would ever make boards again, and I thought about the bullies we had wanted to beat up, and Krubuchek who the Czech policemen killed by mistake. I thought about being in jail, and being alive, and wondered what was going to happen next. Revenge, I decided, was a terrible thing, and this was a terrible situation which could never be fixed, even if everybody knew the whole truth. Even if we all went to confession and said a thousand Hail Mary's and lit a thousand candles. There was nothing to be done.

I decided then to do something about the things I could do something about, and not worry about the things I couldn't do anything about. Ahead of us, there was plenty to be done.

Gunter and Dolfi

CHAPTER 7

Relocation

Some of our neighbors left town. I remember my mother saying goodbye to people, and wishing God would bless them and good luck. One day a family would live in a house, and the next day the house would be empty. We heard terrible stories about something the government was doing called relocation, but there were so many terrible stories. My father told us not to believe everything we heard. He didn't want to talk about it. Nobody talked about it.

We struggled every day just to find something to eat and to help the people who needed help more than we did. We couldn't have imagined how this new government wind would blow three million people into East and West Germany and just leave them there. But that is what happened.

One day Vati came home and told us we were going on a trip. He and my mother had four knapsacks, traveling bags you carried on your back. Mutti and Vati made big piles of our things on the floor, and then made the piles smaller, then smaller. They argued about it, and we weren't allowed to ask any questions. Gunter and I watched and listened.

"Fifty kilos," said my father. "No more. That's what they said."

"Impossible, " said my mother. "The children have to have their clothes. And what is the government going to do with our things when we leave?"

"I don't know," said Vati. "But it's better that we decide what to take than leave it up to them. If we take too much, they'll burn it. That's what they said."

"Do I take what I love?" asked Mutti, "or do I take what might have value to somebody else, if anybody ever has money again?"

"Take what you need to stay alive," said Vati. "Body and soul."

My mother was crying. She took a pair of her shoes out of one pile and picked up a heavy-framed photograph. "This has to go," she said. "I cannot leave it behind." She slid the metal stays off the back and removed the picture. She slipped it between the pages of our big black Bible with the crackled leather cover.

"Good," said my father. "Take what you can't bear to leave behind. Fifty kilos is not much."

They were up all night sorting and rearranging and arguing about the piles of things. My mother had a little bit of jewelry left. It went into the pile and went back off again. All the household things stayed on their shelves. All the books too.

They rolled clothes into tiny little balls and shoved them into the knapsacks. In the morning when Vati woke us up, all our clothes were laid out for us to put on: three pairs of underwear each, three pairs of socks, shorts and pants both, two shirts, a sweater and a heavy coat. We objected, and said we would look like mushrooms and everyone would laugh at us. Vati just told us to be quiet. He said everybody would look like mushrooms and nobody would be laughing. He promised.

We ate everything that was left in the apartment. My mother stood in the kitchen looking at the things still on the shelves. My father handed us our knapsacks. I had to help Gunter with his. We looked at the piles of things still heaped around our house.

"What about those things?" I asked.

"We don't need them," said my father.

"Yes we do," I said. "How are we going to cook?"

"We will find a way to do that when we get where we are going," he said. "Don't worry."

Gunter said, "Where are we going?"

"We are going into West Germany," said my father.

"Why?" said Gunter.

"Because everybody is going. The government says we have to go."

"When are we coming back?"

"I don't know," said Vati.

"I don't want to go," said Gunter. "I want to stay here."

I said nothing. I watched my mother. Her face was blank. I watched her pick up a spoon, just a tiny little one with nothing special about it. It was just a little teaspoon that had perhaps fed baby boys their medicine, or stirred cups of tea for visiting friends, or rapped on the side of a tinkling glass for attention to the toast. She tried to shove it into her knapsack but it was impossible. I watched her struggle to make a space that was not there, and pull it out again, bent around the fingers of her hand. She carried it like this. She would not let it go.

My father looked at his pocket watch, then tucked it into his pants pocket, already bulging with things. "We have to go now boys," he said. "It's 7:00 a.m. The policeman told us we have to be ready to go at 7:00."

He herded Gunter and me out the door, then took my mother's elbow and led her through. He did not lock the door. A big truck was grumbling down the street and we and our neighbors shuffled onto it. It was hot and crowded; our packs were heavy, but we didn't say a word. We looked at our neighbors, just like Vati had said, all bundled up like mushrooms and carrying their packs. Nobody talked to each other. Nobody laughed.

The truck took us to a place near the railroad station, and my father went ahead to speak to the Czech officers. They talked for a while and there was a lot of pointing and hand waving going on. My father seemed to be asking a lot of questions.

He was shaking his head when he came back to talk to us. Vati apparently was in charge of all of us, and he spoke to the other fathers and told them not to worry. They would keep us together here in Mährish-Schönberg for now, until enough people were collected to make a trainload. Then we would be moved to a *Flüchtlingslager*, a camp in Augsburg, West Germany (Bavaria) and held there for transport to Donauwörth. From there we would be assigned and delivered to our permanent relocation areas. Ours would very likely be Oppertshofen, a small village in Bavaria.

After a few days, the guards came to round everyone up and load them on big trucks, *Lastwagen,* for the trip to Augsburg. The men asked questions. My father translated for them. Yes, the families would stay together. No, the *Flüchtlingslager* was only temporary. Yes, we would be fed and provided for. No, there was nothing to worry about.

"Now please," said my father. He looked at his watch. "Let's get on with it in an orderly manner. It is time to go."

We looked at our town, and for the first time realized it was not ours and had never been. It belonged to somebody else, somebody who didn't want us to live there anymore. My mother was crying. All the women were crying. I wanted to cry too, but Vati looked at me and his face was strong and tough.

"What are we going to do?" I asked. "Where are we going to live?"

"It doesn't matter where you live," my father said. "You live, you meet the people there, you work. You make the best of it."

He wanted me to be tough too, so I didn't say anything else. I just watched as the truck motor grumbled through the gears and picked up speed, and everything I knew was left behind.

None of this made any sense to me, but as badly as I wanted to ask Vati about it, I could tell by the look on his face that there had been enough questions. I tried to think of this as just another change in my life, a big change which I could do nothing about. Maybe understanding would come later.

Maybe not.

We didn't stay long in Augsburg. The *Flüchtlingslager* was tolerable I suppose. I don't remember much about it. We were fed and sheltered, and given a place to bathe. We were often hungry, but we were used to being hungry by now, and we were not mistreated, despite the rumors of terrible things happening to other people in other camps in other places. We were together with people we knew, and we listened to my father say that everything was going to be all right.

In a few weeks we were loaded onto trucks again and shipped to Donauwörth where we stayed about four months until the German government found places for our relocation.

Late one night, the officers woke my father up and he woke all of us. It was 1:00 in the morning, and once again it was time to go. Mutti, Vati, Gunter and I, along with the Kunz family and another family named Köhler were trucked off in a *Lastwagen* to Oppertshofen. We were handed over to a farmer there who would give us food and a place to sleep in exchange for work. The Kuntz's had two boys and one girl, and the other Köhler's had two boys.

The Bavarian farmer was not much happier than we were about the situation. I learned later that Bavarians didn't like Germans, even though we hadn't been German for two or three governments back, and started off as something else altogether. He and his family called us *Rucksack Bayern* (Knapsack Germans) which was not a nice thing to be called.

We dropped our packs on the floor of the one room we would share and looked at each other. I didn't understand any of it. It was like the war was still going on, only now we were the enemy. People didn't like us because of where we came from, which we had no choice about. And the truth was we didn't come from anywhere, which we had no choice about either.

My father could not help me understand. "People are people," was all he said. "At least we have a roof over our heads. Be grateful for that."

My mother opened up her pack, removed the big black Bible and set it on a stool. On top of that she placed her bent spoon. "Let's try to go to sleep," she said. "Only God knows what might happen in the morning."

NOTE: May 8, 1945 was VE (Victory in Europe) Day. On May 12, the city of Prague was liberated, signaling the end of military operations in Europe, and the US and Soviet forces began to withdraw. On June 5, the Allies divided Germany and Berlin into East and West, and on

July 16 the Potsdam Conference began. Pre-occupation borders were restored to Bohemia/Moravia and Slovakia; Ruthenia was ceded to the USSR, and three million Germans were systematically expelled from the restored Czechoslovakia.

The Köhler family in Bavaria, 1949

CHAPTER 8

The Farm

My life had changed again. Now we belonged to the farmer, and we were to be farm people instead of city people. My parents, I suppose, had more experience with farms than I did. I think they knew better than Gunter and I how much hard work was ahead of us. To me, after my initial stubborn insistence that it wasn't fair and I wanted to go home, to me it looked like it would be a great adventure.

There were so many animals. Huge Belgian workhorses lived in the barn and hundreds of pigs wallowed in the mud of their own little village. Chickens scratched in the yard and cats roamed around for mice and handouts. Hunting dogs yipped up and down long pens and slow, big-eyed cows grazed with their calves in the fields surrounding the compound. It was an amazing place to me.

The first morning, my mother immediately got up when the rooster crowed and went to work. Somehow she knew exactly what to do, and I was very impressed with this. I followed her around, trying to help and learn as much as I could as quickly as I could.

We went with the farmer's wife into the dark, musky barn. She took a little stool and a bucket and squeezed milk from the sleepy cows, who made grateful moo-sounds and shuffled their big feet. We sneaked into chicken coops and my mother stole eggs from under the hens without even waking them up. Then we went into the kitchen and she put on an apron to help the farmer's wife cook breakfast. After their family had finished, then we were allowed to have something. My mother did the dishes, cleaned the kitchen, and continued to help the farmer's wife all day. I tried to help, but when I got too much in the way she told me to go and watch Gunter, which I was grateful to do.

I explored, as much as I dared, tobacco fields and potato patches, and got myself into serious trouble by eating unripe vegetables from the garden. Gunter told on me, of course, and in addition to a stomach-ache I got a stern lecture from my father that I never forgot.

"This is not our farm," he said. "We came to live with these people and we will do things the way they do things. We have moved into their country, not the other way around. When you go to someone else's home, you follow the rules of their house. Do you understand?"

"I was hungry," I said.

"We are all hungry," said my father. "It makes no difference. We will work for our food and then we will eat. We will not steal from these people, and we will live the way they live. That is the only way to get along in a new place."

At that time, animals were more important than money or people. And food was more important than that. The farmer who housed us raised cows, chickens and pigs. He also grew tobacco, which was another very valuable crop. He planted crops to sell and crops to eat, and to feed the animals. And although we had dairy cattle for milk and butter, we were not allowed to eat the beef. The government had strict restrictions. We were not permitted to breed horses, only the military could do that, but we could eat the horse meat when it was available. Many times Mutti gave me the job of standing in line to buy a pound of horse meat so she could make *goulasch*.

The farm also had a sawmill and a flour mill. But what they had more of than anything else was work. It seemed like we all worked from dark morning to dark night and it was never done, but started over every day. Work was life now. And I did my share.

After six or eight weeks we moved again. My parents had arranged to stay in the same house with the Kuntz family, though we continued working on the farm. We shared four rooms and two bathrooms, and the four of us boys slept up in the attic together. When the weather was cold we would wake up freezing in the middle of the night. The windows frosted over with slowflake patterns of ice, and the blankets were crunchy with cold. I could see the breath of the other boys like a little fog in the attic.

My father looked for work in Donauwörth, and soon got a job as a *lagermeister,* the man in charge of the storage room for the iron-works. Early every morning he took the bus into town and came home after dark. My mother did the cooking for the household, which pleased everyone since she was such an excellent cook. This was lucky because there wasn't a lot of choice about what to eat. My mother's delicious sauces, her specialty, made the difference between a good meal and, almost, preferring to go hungry.

Every day I walked to school in the village of Oppertshofen with the other children. It was a one-room schoolhouse where all eight grades were taught together. I had been out of school for two years because of the war, so the teacher decided to move me up into the fifth grade. It didn't take long to get used to the classroom routine again, although I much preferred to be with the farm animals.

After school I rushed home to get to work. I cleaned the stalls of cows and horses and cleaned the chicken coops. I helped the *schweinezüchtung,* the man who cooked for the pigs. He was an Italian prisoner of war, displaced like us, and it was his job to take the garbage from the house and cook it into proper pig slop so the pigs wouldn't get diseases. I had never heard of such a thing, a restaurant for the pigs, but he worked very hard, like everyone else did and seemed content with his customers.

He had one huge boar that must have weighed 500 pounds. He was so big he broke two of the sows' backs when they tried to breed. It made the farmer so angry he had him castrated and when that didn't work he slaughtered him. I think the pig chef missed the giant boar. He must have been very proud to have fattened him up to such a size.

I also helped the veterinarian, Doktor Karl Niklasch, a man I admired from the first moment I saw him. He wasn't very big, a little more than five feet tall, but powerful, with very big arms. He could do anything with animals and I watched his every move, asking as many questions as I dared and trying to remember everything he said.

"Why do you castrate the little boars, Herr Doktor?" I asked

"So that they won't breed," he said.

"Why?"

"Because we don't want piglets from this one," he said. "We only want the best boars to make babies."

"Why?"

"Because the best pigs are the best ones to eat. If we let all of them breed, we'll have too many to feed, and not enough to eat."

I watched him pull a calf out of a bellowing cow, and cut the horns off a monstrous bull in the pen. I watched him give medicine to the dog and set his broken leg. I watched him explain to a sad farmer that his horse could not be saved, and I watched him explain it to the horse and pat her neck with his big strong hands before he put her down.

It was not an easy job. He used a tool called an *abbattoir* which looked like a gun, that banged a big spike between the animal's eyes. It killed them pretty soon. Afterwards, he had to pull it out. And I had to help clean up the mess. But I would have done anything for him.

This then was my introduction to the processes that made life work. Sex. Life and death. Taking care of the animals that provided food for you. It was hard, but it all made sense to me and in some ways I was happy to be a part of it, doing the boy's work I could do now and getting ready to do the man's work later.

One day, after the second harvest of the hay field, the farmer let the cows out to graze over where the hay was cut. Four of the cows got into some fence wire and ate that along with the hay. It got into their stomachs and made them very sick and bloated. Dr. Niklasch came, but he was not optimistic about saving the cows.

"I'll have to operate," he told the farmer. "I'll make an incision behind the last rib here," he patted the soft brown side of the sick cow, "and try to reach in and remove the wire with a magnet. I'm going to need some help." He looked at me, and nodded. He stroked the cow's neck soothingly. "We'll start with her, and if this works, we may be able to help the others."

I was extremely proud to be asked to help. We tied the cow down and he gave her medicine to put her to sleep. I helped him disinfect his whole arm and watched him make a slice in her side with his scalpel. He reached into her stomach and found nothing. He pushed his hand in farther. There was blood everywhere. He struggled to push his muscular arm in deeper, but it was just too big and it wouldn't fit. He pulled back, frustrated. He wiped the sweat from his forehead with his other arm, and swore. Then he looked at me.

"Dolfi," he said. "Your arm will fit in there."

The room began to spin just a little bit, and my own stomach flopped. I looked at all that blood and tried to imagine the feeling inside a cow's stomach.

For a second I thought I'd run away, but I did not. I was there and I could do it. He poured disinfectant on my arm and I put on a long rubber glove. He gave me the magnet. I held my breath and reached inside as far as I could.

"Gently, now," said Dr. Niklasch. "Move the magnet around slowly. Can you feel anything?"

The truth is I could not. I could only feel squishing like a handful of mud and I tried not to think about it.

"All right, pull it out," he said.

To my amazement, there were fragments of wire on the magnet.

"Excellent," he said. "Now do it again."

I kept working for what seemed like hours, until the magnet came out clean and the doctor needed to stop her bleeding. He sewed up her hide and packed the cut with bandages. "She'll wake up in a while," he said. "Now let's see to the next one."

We worked on the cows all day. We didn't eat and we didn't rest, and we saved three of the cows. On the fourth one, even I couldn't reach the wires in her stomach. It had been too much time and they had passed too far. He explained it to her, and then he shot her with the *abbattoir*. She never made a sound.

I was exhausted when he patted me on the shoulder and thanked me like a man. He said I was the best assistant he ever had.

"Thank you, Doktor Niklasch," I said.

"You're welcome, son," he said. "By the way, what is your actual name?"

"Adolf," I said. "My mother calls me Dolfi."

"Well, in Bavaria, all the men named Adolf are called Adi. Did you know that?"

"No."

"How would you like it if we called you Adi from now on?"

"I think I'd like that very much."

That night up in the attic I lay awake for a long time, thinking. For the first time, I saw a future ahead of me and I knew what I wanted to be when I grew up. A veterinarian. Doktor Adi Köhler. The man who takes care of the animals. I couldn't wait to let my mother know.

"That's very nice, Dolfi," she said the next morning. "That is a wonderful thing for a young man to want to be. And I'm proud of you for helping Doktor Niklasch. He says you did an excellent job, a job nobody else could have done."

"I'm going to work with him every day," I said. "I'm going to learn everything about animals, and everyone will call me Doktor Köhler."

"You'll be the best vet in Bavaria," she said. "Now go and get me some eggs."

"I want to tell Vati," I said. "Wait until I come back."

I ran out to the coop and robbed the hens lightning-fast. I ran by the barn to check on my patients, who were up on their feet looking tired but alive, and that elated me even more. I came back with a whole dozen eggs and the good news.

My father was at the breakfast table with his coffee.

"The cows are on their feet!" I told him. "They're going to be fine."

"Very good," he said. "Sit down, Dolfi."

I gave my mother the eggs. She turned her back to the table and continued her cooking. I sat down with my father.

"I'm going to be called Adi from now on," I said. "Doktor Niklasch says that in Bavaria all the men named Adolf are called Adi."

He looked at me sideways. "Is that so?"

"Yes," I said. "And you always told me that when we are in someone else's country, that we need to do things the way they do."

"All right, *Adi,*" he said. "Sit down please."

I thought he wanted me to tell him the story and I couldn't wait to begin. "You should have seen it, Vati," I said.

"Yes," he said. "You did an excellent job. That's what your mother tells me."

"It was amazing," I said. "We put a magnet into their stomachs and pulled the wires out."

"Your mother also tells me you want to be a veterinarian," he said. He sipped his coffee.

"Yes I do," I said. "I've decided that is what I want to be."

He sipped again, and looked me in the eye. I felt very grown up. "I want you to forget about that," he said.

"What?"

"Do you have any idea how difficult it is to become a doctor? Even an animal doctor takes many years of school and training and a great deal of hard, hard work."

"I can work," I said. "I love animals. That is what I want to do."

"Impossible," he said. "We will never have the money for that kind of education."

I looked at him in amazement.

"You will just be disappointed if you carry on with this crazy idea," he said. "I want you to get it out of your mind. That is the best thing to do."

"No it isn't," I said.

"We will give you what education we can. When we have enough money we are going to open a restaurant and you will work for me."

"I won't," I said.

My mother turned around. "Don't argue with your father," she said.

So that was that. I left the room without saying another word. I had brought my dream to the breakfast table and was taking it back out with me, barely tasted. The feeling stung like metal fragments in my own stomach.

This would not keep me from loving animals. And it would not keep me from having other dreams, or other disappointments for that matter. And for a while I hated my father for crushing my bright ideas of the future. But eventually I came to know that that's what fathers sometimes have to do. They have to think about what's best for everyone. They have to teach sons to be realistic about the world. And mothers have to go along with them, sometimes.

Sometimes we have to do what we have to do instead of what we want to do. Sometimes we have a choice. Sometimes we don't. There would be a time when I didn't have to do what my father said, but that would happen when I was a man. And the only way to be a man, apparently, was to work hard and learn fast. I set about the business of doing this with determination. And I tried to remember that if I ever was a father, my children would be allowed to dream whatever they wanted to dream. And I would help them make their dreams come true.

At least I'd let them live till after breakfast.

CHAPTER 9

Treibjagd

I always cared about animals, sometimes more than people. But I fell in love with horses, a passion which stayed with me throughout my life.

The first horses I got to know were four enormous Belgians who belonged to the Meyer family. They lived across the road from where we lived with the Kuntzes. The Meyer farm had a sawmill and a flour mill, which Herr Meyer ran with his two sons, Otto and Theo. They also bred cattle and pigs.

The family was nice to us, and they adopted us Knapsack Germans as friends. In fact Herr Meyer gave me a job. Not for money, but for food. If I helped his sons all day, I could take home a dozen eggs and some milk in exchange for my labor.

On Saturdays and in the summertime, I walked to the Meyer's farm early in the morning and helped the Meyer boys hitch up the wagon to the big Belgian team. I climbed up on the tongue of the wagon and balanced across it to the lead horse, then scrambled up onto a little pad just behind his withers. We drove out to one of the neighboring farms, loaded up with logs or sacks of grain and took them back to the mills for processing. In a few days we returned to deliver flour or lumber and pick up another load of raw material.

In the soft dark of pre-dawn, the lead horse's broad back was pretty comfortable, and if the farm was far enough away, I could catch a nap, rocking over his shoulders and listening to the rhythmic rumble of his hoofs underneath.

It was heavy work, and the farmer's sons were raised on it. They did all the lifting and hauling, which left me to take care of the horses all day. Whenever we stopped to trade wheat or wood, I climbed down to feed and water them. I scooped the manure up and tossed it off the roadside. Then I had to pick up each one of those sixteen huge feet and clean them properly. They were patient animals, but it was like being in a forest in-between their sturdy forelegs, a forest that could just as easily have spooked and run me over without a hint of warning.

I talked to the horses and calmly, quietly made them understand what I needed them to do. "Easy," I said in a low voice, "let me see your foot."

If we had to move the wagon I directed them very soothingly. "Slow down a little, now. There's no need to rush. Go slow. That's a good boy, now." They responded to the gentleness in my voice, without ever knowing that that was my one and only management strategy, and we grew to be good friends in a short time working together.

In the fall, another one of my jobs was to let the cattle out to graze and bring them in again in the evening. As usual, we were up before dawn, and as soon as the milking was done I untied twenty or thirty of the cows and let each one out of their individual stalls. Once out of the barn, they always ended up following a lead cow, and I had to convince the lead cow to graze in the pasture where the grass was growing.

I did this all by myself, without the help of a dog or a horse to ride on. And I usually ended up at the end of the line, following the cow trail and avoiding what they dropped along the way. We always managed to get where we needed to go, and to get back home the way we came in time for supper.

In addition to my duties for Herr Meyer, I also helped Herr Hans Hetzer with his animals. Herr Hetzer was a *Jägermeister,* someone licensed by the government for hunting in the woods. I helped him take care of his Wirehaired Dachshunds, which he used for hunting badgers and foxes. The dogs were funny-looking little creatures, but fierce, and no other breed of dog was better at routing a badger out of his lair. That was how they got their name in fact, because dachs means badger in German.

They went crazy when they scented a badger, and I enjoyed watching them go. It was amazing to see these friendly, hand-licking, tail-wagging friends of mine turn into snarling and ferocious hunters when they cornered their quarry. Sometimes they came home with bloody noses and chewed-up ears, but it never made them scared to go after the next one.

Sometimes I went with them on the hunt, but they couldn't convince me to carry a gun after my experience in the jail. It was my job, then, to take care of the dogs and to hold them back until Herr Hetzer said to release them. This wasn't always easy, since at age twelve I only weighed about eighty pounds, but I managed.

One day Herr Hetzer organized a *treibjagd,* a big hunt. Late in the fall after the first frost came, a dozen or so volunteers got together out in the field. They lined up shoulder-to-shoulder across a wide area of brush. The hunters with their rifles were on either end. I was in the middle with Hetzer's dogs. We stepped in line across the width of the field to flush the game animals out. Whatever was there, badger, fox, deer, rabbit, wild pigs, were forced to run out both sides, away from the center, giving the hunters a clear shot.

We were at it for a while, and we had already shot our first fox. The dogs were very excited and it was all I could do to hold them. It was a bright day, and everybody was feeling good about the hunt. We were alert and walking carefully, anxious as the dogs to see what would appear next.

All at once we flushed a herd of wild boars. The dogs went berserk. Before I could brace myself, they launched after the boars, dragging me through the brush like Ben Hur without a chariot. I held on for all I was worth.

Don't let go, don't let go. That was all I could think, but my weight barely slowed them down. Guns fired. The dogs yelped like mad. The boars squealed and scattered. The hunters were yelling something I couldn't make out. Something poked me in the eye, but I clamped my fingers tighter on the leashes. They fired again.

I don't know what made the dogs stop, but it was entirely their decision. Herr Hetzer was very pleased that I didn't let go. He slapped me on the back and said "Good job, son. If you'd let the dogs go we might have shot them. And look at the size of this boar, he would have torn up the dogs for sure." The hunters all agreed. They brushed the leaves out of my hair and gave me something to drink from a flask. It was strong and warm and helped wash the dirt out of my mouth.

I was very excited and very proud. We'd gotten several of the boars and a deer, and they promised me some of the boar meat and the venison too. I couldn't wait to tell Mutti about the hunt. I ran all the way home.

When my mother looked at me, she nearly fainted.

"What happened to your eye?!" she said.

"Nothing," I said. "A thorn poked me in the eye, that's all."

"*Gott im Himmel,* look at yourself," she said.

She took me in the bathroom and made me look in the mirror. My eye was completely gray. No pupil, no iris, no white at all. Just gray. I closed my other eye and realized I couldn't see. It didn't hurt at all, but it looked horrible. My poor mother was beside herself.

"I told you not to go out on the *treibjagd*. I told you it was dangerous." She tried putting some kind of ointment on my eye. I didn't feel a thing. "You are too small to go out hunting with the men!"

When Gunter saw my eye, he was impressed. "You look like a monster," he said. "It's horrible." He couldn't stop staring at me. The next day Mutti took me to the doctor. He looked and looked and finally told us I was very very lucky not to lose the eye. Of course I was lucky, like always.

CHAPTER 10

Zum Rübezahl

By 1948, when I was twelve, we learned that if there's anything Bavarians love, it's good food and draft beer. And now that the war was retreating behind us, my mother found a few more ingredients to cook for the farmer's family. They looked forward to her dinners, bragged to their friends how well fed they were, and enjoyed being teased about the extra weight around their middles.

In the spring, there was talk all over town about a big wedding coming up. One of Herr Hetzer's daughters, Anna, was getting married to a nice gentleman with a good-sized farm in Oppertshofen. It was going to be a huge party and everyone was invited. Mutti, acknowledged as the town's best cook, was asked to prepare the food for the wedding. And when they found out my father had been a waiter, well the whole banquet fell into my parents' laps.

My father found an old tuxedo, and my mother spent days, with me along to do the carrying, scouring through the markets for all the freshest vegetables and the very best meats. This wasn't an easy task because food was still a very important commodity. Nothing was allowed to go to waste, and nobody ever had to say "clean your plate." We were grateful for whatever we had.

People used every part of an animal except hoofs and teeth, whatever animal they could get hold of. In addition to the game the *Jägermeister* brought in from the *Treibjagd*, we might have *Taube* (dove) or *Truthahn* (turkey). We weren't allowed to eat the horses after the war was over, since they were too important for transportation.

Even so, my mother managed to cook all the Bavarian favorites: *Knoblauch Suppe* (garlic soup), *Gruner Salat* (green salad), *Schweine Braten* (roast pig), *Rinds Rouladen* (beef rolls), *Beuscherl Saur* (all the insides of a pig), all served with *Nudeln* (noodles) or *Kartoffel* (potatoes).

Mutti was the best saucier, she made everything delicious with her wonderful sauces. That's what really separated her cooking from everybody else's, no matter what she found to cook.

For the wedding, she also baked a cake like nothing I had ever seen before. It was beautiful, almost as tall as Gunter, and decorated all over with flowers. I had no idea my mother could do something like that, and I was so proud of her.

The wedding was a huge success. Everyone had a wonderful time and couldn't stop talking about it for weeks after. They were all saying we should open a restaurant. The next thing I knew, we did. And life changed again.

My father brought in a couple of his friends who were carpenters and they started hammering and sawing away in a bedroom of the house. I helped carry boards in and out and tried to stay out of the way. I watched in amazement as out of nothing, it seemed, grew three corner tables with benches, two tables for four in the middle, and a little bar with three stools.

My father was ecstatic. It was like the days before the war, when his friends would drink beer together and Vati would make everyone laugh. "We're going to call the place Zum Rübezahl," he announced when the carpenters finished.

"What kind of a name is that?" I asked.

"You were too little to remember," said my father. "Rübezahl, the Watcher in the Woods. He was a magic Gnome who lived deep in the Riesen Gebirge, a long, long time ago, even before Kris Kringle was born."

"Kris Kringle always comes at Christmas," I said. "There was nobody before him." I didn't like the name.

My father laughed again. "Oh yes there was," he said. "But that is a story all by itself." He looked at his friends. They remembered; they settled back with their beers. "Rübezahl lived by himself for many, many years. He had magical powers and could create whatever he wanted from the things he found in the woods, the flowers, nuts, roots, berries and bark from the trees. But he was very lonely.

"One day he saw a beautiful Princess playing with her friends by a pool of water. He wanted her for his wife, so that night he left the forest, sneaked into her castle and stole her for himself. To try and make her happy, he collected a basket full of beets and turned them into her playmates. Then he turned other things into anything she wanted, and she finally promised to marry him.

"But the Princess was crafty too, and she played a trick on Rübezahl. She told him she wanted lots and lots of wedding guests. He went out into the field and started counting the beets so he could turn them into people for the wedding. But there were so many that while he was gone, she ran away and married another man."

Vati stopped and took a long drink from his stein. I said, "That's not a happy ending. I don't like it. And I don't like the Princess and I don't like girls."

"Oh you'll change your mind about that," said Vati. Everyone laughed. "Just like Rübezahl. At first he was furious, and wanted to destroy everything he saw in the woods. But he decided to forgive her because of his true love. Instead, he used his magic to make beautiful things, toys and presents for the children. Then each year at Christmastime, he would sneak into the village and leave a surprise for every child, hoping one day to give a gift to hers."

Vati waved his arms around the room that was his new restaurant. "And this will be like Rübezahl for us. We made it out of whatever we had, and it's going to bring us everything we want. And starting from today, we're going to celebrate every day of the year like it's Christmas." He held his glass up for a grand toast. "To Rübezahl," he said.

I didn't think it was possible, but it happened before my eyes. In just a few days all the neighbors had come to paint the walls with scenes from the Riesen Gebirge with the mountains in the background. Each wall was like a page out of a fairy tale.

And customers came in the door as soon as the paint was dry. My mother cooked good old-fashioned Bavarian food and my father served up foaming steins of beer and glasses of wine from the region. On Sundays he brought in a keg of fresh beer from the brewery and everybody came in for their *frühschoppen* (an early beer after Church).

Immediately, I was a busboy. And a dishwasher. And a bartender too when it was busy. And occasionally a cook, when I helped my mother by putting the *wurst* in the water to cook, or stirring a sauce or peeling endless piles of *Kartoffel*. I much preferred the animal work to the restaurant business, but my father needed the help. He still had his *lagermeister* job in the daytime, and as soon as he got home he went right away to the dining room. So, after school Gunter and I did the same thing. We worked hard, and learned fast. Empty glasses were unacceptable. As soon as a table was empty it had to be cleaned for the next guest. And there was always a next guest. We learned to eat our own meals standing up in a corner of the kitchen, wolfing everything down in a hurry so we could get back on the floor.

At Zum Rübezahl, the daily menu usually had one or two hot items, like *Gebackenes Hühnchen* (baked chicken), *Sauere Leber* (sour liver) or *Wiener Schnitzel* along with soup (oxtail was a favorite). We also had a cold plate, sausages, lots of bread and rolls, and butter if we could get it. On rare occasions we'd serve *Kalbfleish* (veal) or *Matjes Herring* (fish). Mutti was now famous for her sauces, and people said she could make an old shoe taste good. Vati laughed when they said that, and threatened to put it on the menu.

On the weekends we did something wonderful at Zum Rübezahl, something the people hadn't seen in a long time. We made ice cream. It was my job to chip the ice and crank and crank the big steel freeze machine for hours until the custard froze. Then we'd run a red and white flag that said *"Eis"* up the pole outside. Everybody in the neighborhood came then and paid five pfennig for a scoop, until the last of it was scraped up off the bottom of the can.

In 1949, I completed eighth grade and started going to *Handelschule,* business high school, which was intended to give a young man a good start on a good job. I knew if I couldn't be a veterinarian, and I didn't want to slave in the restaurant for the rest of my life, I was going to have to learn to do something else. I took every class I could, accounting, typing, shorthand and all kinds of business practices. I worked very hard in *Handelschule,* as hard as I did in the restaurant.

It wasn't easy. I rode my bike thirteen kilometers each way to school and back. In the winter I would arrive there half frozen and soaking wet. If the bike broke down, I either had to hope I'd brought the right tool along to fix it, or pray that the next truck would pick me up and give me a lift home.

Zum Rübezahl was such a success that in 1951 my father was asked to take over a restaurant in Donauwörth. It was called Kaffehaus (Coffee House), and owned by the Sixen Brau brewery. We were provided living quarters there, and it was just across from my school, so I didn't have to bicycle all that way before going to work. It was a much bigger, nicer place, with a big *Saal* (reception area) upstairs, and lots of tables and a long bar downstairs.

It even had something I had never seen before, a *Kegelbahn,* a bowling alley, right inside the restaurant. Now Gunter and I had a new job. We perched in a little corner on the side while the men rolled the heavy wooden balls down the lane. Then we ran out to set all the *kegel* back up for them to do it again. At first it was a game. But after doing this all weekend long till midnight, we got tired of it. Even washing the bar glasses was a break.

Somewhere along the way, I had an inkling that I might like to be in the hotel business. I don't know where the idea came from, but it wouldn't leave me alone after that. I started putting together a plan for what I wanted to do. But I wasn't ready to share it with my father, not just yet.

My father was a tough boss, a perfectionist. And although he never asked me to do anything he wouldn't do himself, he did so much it was impossible to keep up. Between him and school, I never had a minute of my own time.

But in the summer, whenever I could sneak away, I loved to go swimming in the Danube. I was there so often the boys made me one of their Junior Assistant Lifeguards. It was the first job title I ever had, and I took the responsibility very seriously. Whenever I got the chance I was at the river, parading up and down with my new whistle, ever watchful for a swimmer, with any luck a female swimmer, in distress.

I had learned how to swim a few years earlier in Opportshofen. Nobody had time to teach me, but this was something I was determined to do, so I did. I went down to the little river, the Kessel, that crossed the back of the farm, undressed, and waded in. I was not afraid of the water, but I hadn't thought it would run so fast or be so cold. I looked at the opposite bank, took a deep breath and started to walk until it was deep enough for me to paddle like a dog. I didn't get far across. But I did get pulled half a kilometer downstream and have to walk all the way back to find my clothes. The next day I tried it again, and by the end of the summer I could make it all the way across and back seven times. Seven was my lucky number, and swimming was my first conquest.

The Danube was very different from the Kessel. It had a strong, fast current which created a whirlpool in the middle of the river that could suck an inexperienced swimmer down to the bottom. Several people had been lost to the river, and no one was allowed to go close to the area.

After talking about it all summer, the lifeguards decided that some of us Juniors were ready to conquer the vortex. We all swam out together, to where we could see the whirlpool. For a while we watched it spin like a sunken tornado, then I volunteered to go first. I have no idea what possessed me to do it.

I swam out while the others treaded water. When I reached the whirlpool I did what they'd told me to do. I took a big, deep breath, stopped swimming and relaxed. I flattened both arms against my sides and let my feet drop. The cold water swallowed me.

I dropped fast, farther and farther down. The surface of the water darkened above my head. I could hold my breath for a long time, but confidence was leaking out of me faster than air bubbles. Seconds passed. Panic began to ask questions: Is something wrong? How long has it been? What if this doesn't work?

In a moment of doubt, I started to break and kick for the surface. But instead of fighting the current, I fought the thought. I forced myself to be calm and let the water do what it was going to do. I kept thinking soon I'll hit the bottom. Then there's nowhere to go but up.

I waited. My chest heaved and tried to press air into my empty lungs. I squeezed my eyes tighter shut and clamped a hand over my nose and mouth. Nowhere but up.

My feet hit stones. I was at the very bottom point of the funnel. Before I could think, the vicious current grabbed my body and spit it out across the river bottom. Outside of the whirlpool, I pushed off and swam hard. I came up to the surface hearing cheers.

Adi Köhler in Handelschule, business high school, age 15

Vati's biggest restaurant, Sixen Bräu Stüble Und Saal

CHAPTER 11

Waiter days

The next thing to change in my life was myself. I started attending *Handelschule* in 1949 when I was thirteen years old. At that age, as any man will tell you, your body begins to make decisions for itself, sometimes without informing your brain. My voice went first, and Mutti's pride and joy, her solo soprano in the boys' choir, was now a froggy, unpredictable tenor.

About the same time, I discovered the opposite sex were undergoing changes as well. And taking careful note of all those new developments seemed to become my alien body's full time job. There was nothing I could do about it. My curiosity nearly killed me sometimes.

In fact that, finally, was what caused another change in my life: my deviation from the path of a born-and-raised Catholic. It was sex. I just couldn't be convinced that it was a sin. I knew what sex was all about from observing the animals, so the act itself was no big mystery, and I knew there was no way sin was involved. But when the priests tried to tell me that my almost-perpetual state of being, the thoughts that generated that, and my attempts at relief were all sinful, well I had to draw the line. I just didn't see how my feelings could make any difference to God, or how in the world I was supposed to keep everything under control.

I consoled myself by thinking Jesus might have understood, having been a teenager, and I stopped going to church.

It was a little bit of an issue with the family at first, but my father found ways to use my extra time. I was to be a professional waiter.

Compared to the dramatic happenings in my life up to that point, the restaurant was total boredom and endless work. Vati had a plan for me, and I think it never occurred to him that I would question that plan or hesitate to go along with it. He had already made it quite clear that I was not going to be a veterinarian, and that was never discussed again.

"We'll train you the way I was trained," he said. "Exactly so. And after two and a half years of working with me, you'll have your license. You can work for any restaurant in the country." I knew he really meant that I would work for him in his big dream: a succession of bigger and grander restaurants across Europe.

In those days there was not much one could do about a decision like that, and having long since learned not to fight systems which were out of my control, I did the best I could to please him and keep my own dreams under wraps. From what he told me, I must apprentice with a professional for two and a half years, then take a written exam as well as a practical test. Then I would be licensed as Waiter.

For two years, he took me through the paces, from the finer points of tray balancing to the proper pronunciation of French menu items. I wish I had a nickel for every plate I placed on a table full of hungry Bavarians and a dime for every beer I artfully drew from the tap with the correct one-quarter inch head. Every night after school, and day and night on the weekends.

I was a skinny kid, and my arms and legs did not always cooperate with my brain. Over and over again he would drill me. "Who taught you how to walk like that, Dolfi?" He'd stand at the kitchen door and snipe as I approached with a heavy tray. "Stand up straight. Take even steps and keep your feet close to the floor. You're going to trip over everything." And if a pretty girl came in the restaurant, my brain would lose complete control. Vati always noticed.

"Pay attention, Dolfi," he said. "You're splashing beer on the table. You're going to drown the guests before they have a chance to order."

More than anything else, he drilled me to take care of our *Stammgäste* (returning guests), for they made your business. When people showed up after church for their *Frühschoppen,* we would have their drinks on the table before they got their coats off, so that they'd come back the next Sunday. It was endless.

If I wasn't actually serving customers, there was always something to clean. If I wasn't cleaning, I was in the kitchen chopping vegetables or off running an errand for my father, who seemed to require longer and more frequent afternoon naps. If I was in the restaurant, and absolutely everything was done, I had better be on the floor asking guests how they were enjoying their dinner this evening, and how we might improve the menu in the future. And after all that, I had to study.

No more hunting, no more horses, no more exploring in the woods. By day I was studying accounting and stenography, planning a future in a big hotel in a big city. By night I was an automaton in a bow tie, carrying dishes and living up to Vati's expectations.

But I was doing well in *Handelschule.* I excelled in every subject, and always did my assignments despite the long, late hours in the restaurant. When I graduated in 1953, I was ready to take on the world, plus I had almost completed my two and a half year sentence learning waiter. Six more months and then I'd have my official license. With that in my hands, at least I'd have a shot at a job in another restaurant somewhere else. Waiters made good money in big cities. And hotels had good restaurants.

Six months later, we filled out the paperwork, I typed it myself, and sent it in to the government agency. It came back. Denied.

"What does this mean?" I asked Vati.

"It means you haven't been trained, officially," he said.

"What?" I was furious.

"There are stipulations. You were supposed to be going to *Berufschule* (professional school) once a week, in order to stay ahead of those things, your accounting, typing, and so forth."

"But I just graduated! That's ridiculous. We'll write them a letter."

"And there are other stipulations."

"What other stipulations? What else is there to know? You've taught me everything."

My father looked guilty. I had never seen such a look.

"I have taught you everything I know, Dolfi," he said, "but I am not a licensed instructor. It is not acceptable by the agency."

I was thunderstruck. "Then what have I been doing for the last two years?"

"You are an excellent waiter," he said. "But if I am not a licensed instructor, you cannot be certified."

"You mean this whole exercise was just a waste of time?" I could not believe it. My father had lied to me. At best he had misled me, let me believe he was somebody he was not. He had manipulated me. He had let me down. I could not believe it.

He gave me a day off. I spent it sulking and plotting, wishing never to eat in a restaurant again as long as I lived. But once again, there was nothing to be done about the past two years. It was behind me, and now my job was to gather up what I had learned and make the best of it.

And as I learned over and over again in my life, most bad news is good news in a very, very clever disguise.

By the end of the day I was ready to reveal my plan, but I did not go to him first. First, I spoke to Mutti.

She always knew what I was thinking, and she could read the determination in my face as I walked into the kitchen of Kaffehaus. She was taking a rare break, just sitting down with a cup of tea. She looked at the leftover hurt and anger on my face, and I could see she wanted to give me a hug and tell me it would be all right, like when I was a child. Instead, she poured me a cup of tea and asked, "Have you thought everything over?"

"Yes I have."

"And have you decided to forgive your father?"

I avoided her question. "I want to go to *Hotelfachschule*" (hotel school).

She looked at me, taken off guard. *"Hotelfachschule?* Why?"

"I've spent the last two years learning waiter, but I can't be a waiter. I spent three years in the *Handelschule,* but I can't be a businessman." I could tell I was convincing, but I knew I had to win her over completely to have a chance with Vati. "Half of the hotel business is the restaurant business. I'll have a head start on everybody there."

"Yes."

"I wasted all this time trying to do something Vati wanted me to do. And I did the best I could. All my life other people have been telling me what to do and where to live. Now I want to do something for me."

"I see," she said. She sipped her tea.

"And I know this is what I want to do."

She took a moment to look at me. It was the same look she used to give me when she doubted my story, or tried to blame Gunter for something she knew I had done. She wanted to be sure I knew what I was saying.

I did.

"Your father will be disappointed, Dolfi," she said. "He wants you to stay with him in the restaurant."

"I know that," I said. "But you can help me convince him this is the right thing to do."

"Yes," she said, and let her famous smile cross her face. "I can."

There was a lot of talking after that, a lot of which I was not privy to. But in 1953, I was packed up and sent to Willy Kermess Hotelfachschule in München-Pasing. My father had agreed to pay for one year of tuition, 6000 Deutsche Marks (about $1,500). Mutti helped with other expenses until I started making a little money on my own.

It was the first time I would be away from my family. We arrived at the train station very early, and in spite of one or two tears at the platform, I was not afraid. I was ready to be Adi Köhler on his own two feet. I had never been so excited in my life. Of course, those two feet had a lot of walking to do.

Graduation from hotel school, 1954

Adi (third from left) with the Banquet Team at Willy Kermess Hotelfachschule

CHAPTER 12

Hotelfachchule

In München-Pasing, I was picked up by a teacher and delivered to a dormitory that contained about a hundred new students. I shared a room with three other boys, and if we did not become fast friends, we at least worked out the details of life at school and lived together the best we could. The students were from all over Germany. There were no other *Bayern* or local boys. At seventeen and a half, I was the youngest in my class, and therefore subject to a lot of teasing. But I remembered my father's teaching from relocation days and tried to immediately learn the rules and cooperate with my new environment. We lived with a lot of restrictions. There was no drinking or smoking in the dorms, we had to be in bed by 11:00, and absolutely no girls in the dorm. At least those were the rules.

I was required to enroll in a religious class. Since I'd already decided I could not live as a Catholic, I joined the Protestant class, taught by the Reverend Gunter Hochberger. He was a big man with a big smile, not at all like the priests from my previous schools. He had a wife and children, he enjoyed a drink now and then and he didn't have to hide who he was in order to be a Reverend. I was relieved to learn that being a religious person didn't mean you had to give up all the best things in life. Yes, there is a God, but life on earth could be normal, with a mother and father who slept in the same bed.

Our Headmaster was a father-and-son team. Herr Willy Kermess, Sr. was getting on in age so Herr Willy Kermess, Jr. was in charge. He and I got along very well from the beginning. He encouraged me, and I worked hard in all my classes because more than anything else I wanted to succeed in the hotel business. Soon, thanks to another gentleman who was a major influence in my life, I was well on the way.

Viktor Singer was a remarkable man. At seventy years old he was still electrically energetic, and managed to always keep one step ahead of his students. He was a smallish, gray-haired man, always impeccably dressed in a dark suit with a vest, and a wide gray tie with a diamond stickpin. Herr Singer had been Königlicher Servierhofmeister, the service master to King Ludwig II of Bavaria. That made him the most qualified and expert restaurateur in the country. He had an elegant manner and a teaching style that made us want to work hard for him. He took an interest in all of us and was never rude or unreasonable.

His voice was unforgettable.

"No," he would say to us again and again. "You never say 'no' to your guest. Never."

"But, Herr Singer," someone would say, "what if they are asking for something impossible?"

"Nothing is impossible forever," he said. "First ..." and he cracked a classic grin that would melt the heart of the stodgiest Baroness. "First, you smile. Smile, smile, smile. It is your best weapon. Show me."

We would return the grin like idiots.

"Then you apologize. Tell me."

"We're sorry, Herr Singer."

"Oh thank you, Gentlemen." Everyone laughed, and then he got back down to business. "You never say no. You solve the problem without using that word. You offer them something as an alternative. You say you can have the Chef prepare it, but they will have to wait. You say you have no more veal, but you offer an excellent beef dish at a discount. Let them decide what they prefer. But you never say no." Then he asked the class. "Now what did I say?"

"Never say no!" we'd chorus back.

"Bravo!"

At the time, there were a lot of veterans and Prisoners of War coming back to school for training to re-enter the work force. But no one in the school had learned waiter like me, even though I was the youngest. I could polish silver perfectly, do the fancy napkin folds, set the table properly for any menu, and approach a guest with courtesy and skill.

Viktor Singer recognized my training, and took me as his protegé. He toured me through the markets and slaughterhouses, and taught me how much to buy for how many people, how to look for the best of everything, and exactly who and how to ask for what I wanted if it wasn't at the counter.

Soon he picked me out for the school's Banquet Team, along with eight or nine other guys, depending on how big a crew was needed. I was used to hard work and late hours, and I needed the money badly. Almost before I realized what was happening, I was the team captain.

One of the first affairs we worked was at the great hotel the Vier Jahreszeiten (Four Seasons) in Munich. It was a huge banquet for Professor Theodor Heuss, a very high political figure. As we entered through the service doors in our rented tuxedos, I was dazzled by the hugeness of the sparkling kitchens, bustling with crisp-hatted chefs barking orders in French and German to an army of cooks. Cavernous corridors led into a ball room filled with candlelight and violin music, straight out of a Bavarian fairy tale. I was awestruck.

I stood at the doorway staring into the room, imagining the tables filling up. Imagining beautiful ladies in their gowns being seated by elegant gentlemen in tuxedos. I heard the clinking of wine glasses and saw them smiling across the tables to each other. Laughter. I heard the room fill with laughter, as my father's kitchen did a thousand years ago.

Viktor Singer walked up beside me and smiled. I looked at this funny little man with the old fashioned tie bearing the crest of King Ludwig II. He read my mind.

"It's quite a place, isn't it?" he said.

"It certainly is."

"It is one of the finest hotels in the world, Adi," he said. "Take a good look."

"I've been doing that since the moment I walked in the door."

"Very good," he said. "Remember that. And remember this too. If you want to be successful in this crazy business, only work for first-class hotels."

I never forgot his words.

Once inside he turned us over to the Banquet manager for the hotel, a drill sergeant of a man named Herr Walterspiel. He was a ruthless perfectionist, and before any function he lined up the entire service staff and paraded up and down, inspecting.

"Let me see your hands," he barked. We thrust our hands out palms up, then palms down to show what had better be clean fingernails. And no rings.

"Shoes," he said. We lifted the cuff of our pants to show polished black-only shoes.

In German he said, "Share your breath with me." Then he walked the entire line, and if you smelled of garlic you were sent in back to find mouthwash. And if you smelled of booze, you were sent home.

We worked like soldiers, not only at the Vier Jahreszeiten, but at huge elaborate banquets at the Bayerischer Vereins Bank and other elegant ballrooms all over the city. We made a fair amount of money, and for the first time in my life I could put my hand in my pocket and something would be in there. Something I had earned for myself. It was quite a feeling.

CHAPTER 13

Frankfurter Hof

I graduated from Hotelfachschule in 1954 and started looking for a job. With the help of Viktor Singer and Willy Kermess, Jr., I made a list of the finest hotels in Germany, twenty or thirty of them. I found out the names of the proper people to address, and typed each one a letter myself, along with my curriculum vitae. My waiter days would soon be behind me forever, so I thought. No more trays and aprons for me. I had my sights set on *Chef de Reception,* a front desk manager in the gray-striped pants and a vest and jacket. My friends thought I was crazy, shooting too high too fast. "You'll never have a chance," they told me. "Do you know how hard it is to get into places like those?"

Although I got several offers, I was excited to be contacted by Frankfurter Hof, for a job as a *Voluntär* (assistant clerk) at the Front Desk. It was an entry-level position, but to me it was the next big step on the road of my biggest plans, and I packed up and moved to Frankfurt. My new home was the Chauffeur's room in an annex of the hotel, which I shared with three other guys. We made about 110 Deutsch Marks a month (about $25) and took our meals in the cafeteria. I hadn't had such bad food since the war days, but at least I didn't have to pay for it. Just like school, we were all working night and day and there wasn't much time or money for play, but we managed to have fun, as most motivated young men do.

Frankfurter Hof was one of the most prestigious old hotels in Germany. It was owned by General Consul Egon Steigenberger, who we

only saw on very rare occasions. Our two *Chefs de Reception* ran a
tight ship with high service standards that were never permitted to
slip. Pepo Brehm during the day and Herr Karpf on the night shift
were the two toughest bosses I ever had.

They were from the old school, the one which taught that yelling
and screaming at your employees was the surest way to win their
loyalty and ensure success. They were continuously correcting our
work and telling us what to do. And if you ever approached the Front
Desk, there was hell to pay.

"What are you doing here? Go to the back!" Herr Karpf would
command. "You are not ready to come to the Front Desk yet!"

We learned our place very quickly. A *Voluntär* is only an assistant
front desk clerk, an errand boy. It would take at least a year to work
my way up to where I wanted to be. My job at the time was to do all
the guest registrations and keep their history cards up-to-date. This
was very important so that the returning guests received their preferred rooms, and so the *Sekretärs* (Front Desk Clerks) could give
them the proper recognition and welcome them back.

We did all our bookkeeping on the old NCR 2000 machine and it
was my job to assist the *Sekretärs* with the postings. We were only
permitted to carry things back-and-forth to them, never to approach
the Front, until we were properly trained and promoted. So I spent
my days fetching the bills out of the cupboards, adding up the charges
by hand, and delivering them to the man on the NCR 2000 for post-
ing. Then I would run them back to the box. I was running back-and-
forth all day long, but at least it wasn't in a restaurant.

After about six months I also worked the night shift, either 3:00-
11:00 p.m. or 11:00 p.m.-7:00 a.m. I learned how to do the night
audit, and became very proficient on the NCR 2000 with my typing
experience. We also entered everything by hand in a journal, and
made sure it matched the machine totals.

Every charge had to be initialled, and for the first few months we
all signed with a pencil. Then one day Herr Karpf went on the war-
path when he couldn't figure out somebody's signature on an entry.
He stormed in the next morning with a fistful of pens and we were
all assigned a different color.

"No more unaccountable errors," he said. And woe to him who forgot and used the wrong color. My pen was green, and I used a green pen from that day forward.

One time when the hotel was very busy, Pepo asked me to escort a guest to his room. This was unheard-of for a *Voluntär* and I was immediately nervous. I grabbed the key, straightened my lapels and stepped up to greet our guest. He was a smallish oriental-looking gentleman, the first I'd ever met. He said nothing as we walked to his room. When I opened the door, with as much flair as I could muster, I almost closed it and left. This was not one of our best rooms at all, in fact it was more like the Chauffeur's room where I lived than something we would give to our guests. I knew we were busy and we probably had nowhere else to put him, so I decided to make the best of it.

I took him in and tried to communicate an apology on behalf of the hotel, but he didn't speak German and I didn't speak Japanese. I tried saying "I'm sorry" in English. He seemed to understand a little bit, and acted like he appreciated my concern. He shook his head and waved his hand as if to say "It's okay." Then he did something that I'd never seen before. He reached in his pocked and pulled out a little white card. He offered it to me with both hands, and bowed. The card introduced him as Mr. Tetsuzo Inumaru. I nearly dropped it on the floor. Although the card was written in English on one side and Japanese on the other, I realized quick enough that here was one of the most famous hotel men in the world, standing right in front of me. Mr. Inumaru in 1923 opened Frank Lloyd Wright's most controversial building, The Imperial Hotel in Tokyo, and steered it into becoming not only a success, but a legend.

I was completely taken off guard. I had never seen a business card before, or encountered anyone so famous who presented themselves that way. "I am sorry," I said again in English, but he seemed satisfied enough with the room. I immediately went downstairs and cut a little square of paper, typed my name, job title and the hotel address on it. I ran it back up to his room and tapped on the door.

"Mr. Inumaru," I said, "thank you for your card. It is the first I've ever received, and here is mine." I bowed as he had done.

He took it with both hands and read it carefully.

"Oh," he said, "Adi?"

"Yes," I said. "That is my name."

"Arrigato Gozaimashita, Adi-san."

We bowed to each other again. As I backed out the door he was still reading my card.

I received a Christmas card from Mr. Inumaru for almost fifty years. And I always sent one to him, signed in green of course. After his passing, his son Ichiro and I continued to exchange Christmas cards. Ichiro-san was a Cornell graduate, who held several internships in the United States before returning to the Imperial Hotel in 1961 and rising to President and General Manager in 1986. In 1998 he was honored by the Prime Minister of Japan for his many contributions to the Japanese hospitality industry.

Mr. Inumaru's and my paths never crossed again, but somehow we made a connection on his visit to Germany in those long-ago days. The world is a very different place now, but whenever I trade business cards with someone from Japan, in that special two-handed exchange, I remember him.

After about a year as *Voluntär,* I was promoted to *Sekretär* and finally permitted to wear the striped pants and gray vest, and to stand at the Front Desk like a professional. I also got a little bit of a raise, and was able to move out of my quarters and into an apartment within walking distance of Frankfurter Hof. Now I was getting somewhere.

I took great pride in my new position, and I greeted every guest personally, making every effort to be sure their preferences were properly taken care of, which was not always an easy task.

Our guests were strictly upper crust, many dignitaries and celebrities. One time an Arabian prince showed up with his entire service staff of twelve or fourteen people, cooks, maids, and a team of bodyguards who would secure the floor completely. Nobody was allowed to go up on his floor. They even cooked in the hallways, which we very much tried to discourage, but usually left such delicate negotiations up to the General Manager.

In a great hotel like that the clock never stops. Things continue to happen twenty-four hours a day, 365 days of the year, weekends and holidays alike. The GM was not always available. One time when my boss was taking his meal break, I received a frantic call from House-keeping. For some reason the maids refused to clean this particular room. They wouldn't even go inside, and the floor supervisor was insisting they needed a manager to come up. I took the situation upon myself and went up to the room. The supervisor and a gaggle of her maids were waiting timidly outside the door.

The supervisor let me in, and at first nothing seemed out of place. Then we went into the bathroom, and my eyes nearly jumped out of my head. There was something I had never seen before or since, sex gadgets and toys and things I never knew existed. There was quite a collection of rubber body parts, both male and female, some the size a man would only dream about.

"What do we do?" asked the floor supervisor.

"Don't touch anything," I said. It was all I could think of to say. I knew when I was in over my head.

I immediately reversed my decision to take responsibility and called the *Chef de Reception*. He decided to pack everything up and have the room cleaned immediately. When the guest returned, he was politely asked to leave, and to which address would he prefer his cartons mailed? I was impressed with the way he handled the situation with the utmost discretion and respect for the guest's confiden-tiality. "People's preferences behind the bedroom door are their own business," he told me later. "The hotel only provides the bedroom, and the door."

In November 1956, my career was interrupted by a telephone call from my father in Nördlingen, where he was now running an even bigger restaurant. It was owned by the same brewery, and named after it: Sixen Bräu Stüble Und Saal. They were busier than ever.

"Adi, your mother is sick," he said. "And we need you to come home."

I immediately thought the worst. "What is it?" I said. "Is she in the hospital?"

"No, but the doctor says she has to rest."

"Thank God," I said. "I will come and visit as soon as I can get a couple days off."

"No," said Vati. "We need you to come now. Your mother cannot work in the restaurant."

So that was it.

"For how long?" I asked.

"Just for the winter season," he said. "Through Fasching."

"But that's not until March. They'll never let me take that much time off."

"I need you here," he said.

I had to quit my job at Frankfurter Hof. One more time, life had changed and there was nothing I could do about it. But I promised myself it would only be for one season, that this was the last time, and that I would be working at another first class hotel again in the spring. Pepo and Herr Karpf seemed genuinely sorry to see me go. They shook my hand and wished me luck. I stole one of their green pens.

I went back to the restaurant and back under my father's direction, working like the devil through the busy Christmas season and the long, cold months until time for Fasching (also called Karneval or carnival). Fasching began on the Tuesday before Ash Wednesday and carried on day and night. People ate too much, drank too much, and did everything they could to make spectacles of themselves, break all the rules and turn the place topsy-turvy. Everybody wore masks and carried noisemakers, parading up and down the streets in bright, gaudy costumes. They elected Prinz Karneval and a court of fools to govern the village and hand down "sentences" to people they didn't like.

It was a crazy time which I had enjoyed as a boy, but I now I had to work all the way through, and there was no time to join in the fun. It put things in a different light for me. Wild marching in the street in strange clothes. Fool governments that came and went, punishing people at whim. The city turned upside-down, with a mess to be cleaned up after. It reminded me of Mährisch-Schönberg. Those were crazy times too. I did not like the memories. I was anxious to get out of there and back to my career, and I was bored to death.

One Sunday, one of our regular *Stammgäste,* Herr Dettmar, came in for his *Früschoppen*. He was riding his motorcycle. I could hear him revving the engine and spinning gravel in the driveway, so I took a break from the dishes and went out for a look. It was a beauty, a brand-new 250cc BMW. I wanted a ride so bad I could hardly stand it. I couldn't say a word; I just stood there with a big grin all the way across my face, and a soapy, dripping dishcloth in my hands. He pulled in behind a Volkswagen and leaned it over onto the kickstand.

"Good morning, Adi," said Herr Dettmar.

"Good morning, Herr Dettmar. That's a beautiful bike."

"Isn't it something? I just picked it up this week. Come and see."

I stroked the shiny gas tank and patted the leather seat, walked all the way around once, admiring every inch of it.

"Would you like to take her for a ride?" There was a tempting twinkle in his eye. I knew I couldn't; I knew Vati would kill me. "Come on," he said. "Your papa doesn't have to know. Just a quick spin."

I could feel my head nod, the silly grin still on my face. He said, "It's easy, like riding a bicycle. Here." He held the BMW steady and I climbed on. "Your right hand is on the throttle and the left one is the clutch. These are the brakes."

"Where is the gear shift?"

"Your left foot."

"How do you turn it on?"

"Kick the starter down hard."

I did. It growled and shimmied. Her Dettmar was coaching me. "Now give it a little gas, with your right hand." Vati was nowhere in sight. I gunned the motor like I'd been dying to do. *Vroom vroom vroom*. We were ready to roll. "Good!" said Herr Dettmar. "Now shift into first with your foot." So far, so good. "Now slowly release the clutch and give her a little more gas as you go. Easy now."

I concentrated very hard on every step. Gently, slowly I eased the clutch out and opened the throttle at the same time. What I didn't know was that the clutch was adjusted to only release in the last couple of millimeters, so by the time I'd let go, the throttle was wide open. That bike reared up on its hind legs and screeched like a wildcat. It pounced on the Volkswagen, and made it about halfway over in a death-defying leap.

The sound must have been terrible. Everyone came running out of the restaurant to see what was going on. Including Vati. There I was on top of Herr Steinberger's car, trying to wrestle the BMW down. And losing.

Herr Dettmar was laughing so hard I think he hurt himself. I wasn't injured, which was another lesson in good luck, but Vati was going to have to pay for damages to both vehicles. Herr Dettmar said he should have told me about the clutch, and Vati said it could have been a lot worse. I apologized to everyone and volunteered to help with the repairs. They went back inside for another beer, and I promised myself I'd never touch another motorcycle. There was a long stretch of extra work ahead of me—and another big change around the corner.

Kathrin Gutt and Adi in the gardens of Bad Byrmont, 1957

CHAPTER 14

CHACHA

In April of 1957, I landed a good job as a front desk clerk at Das Kurhotel in Bad Pyrmont, where wealthy Europeans came from everywhere to drink the waters, eat the special cuisine, take saunas and massages, and thereby improve their health from head to toe. It was located in a very beautiful park setting, Kur Park, where people strolled through the gardens every afternoon following their spa treatments and consultations by a small army of doctors. This was the first time I'd ever been to an actual spa, and it was a completely different experience. I had never seen so many people have so many things done to themselves, for not much better reason than to learn how to relax.

It was not so much a glamorous place as a health facility, but to me it will always be very special and romantic, because it was there I first met the woman who would be my wife and best friend for the rest of the century and beyond, Kathrin Gutt.

The spa was only open seasonally, so we made the most of it. We worked our eight-hour shift and for once had enough money to go out in the evening. There was a little place, the Spelunken (Cave), in town. It was built downstairs under the street, and it stayed open until 4:00 in the morning. A bunch of us would go there two or three times a week after our shift. We'd have a couple drinks and dance all night long to American-style jazz. It was tremendous fun.

I was never shy on the dance floor; we learned all the latest steps—swing dance and jitterbug, all of them. Kathrin loved to dance. And whether it was with me or another of our friends, she was never in her chair when the band started to play the cha cha cha. That's how she got her nickname, Chacha, which immediately stuck, permanently.

I got a very lucky break at Das Kurhotel one night when the Concierge got drunk. He couldn't come to work, and the manager came to me in a panic.

"What can you do?" he asked. "Do you know anything about being a concierge?"

I had heard about the problem, of course. Gossip always runs through hotels at unbelievable speed. And having a little background in the business, I knew I was up to the job. "I can do whatever you ask," I said calmly. "And I know you never say 'no' to the guest."

He looked me up and down. Maybe he was impressed with my confidence, and maybe he was desperate, but he put me on the desk and the man was fired. I immediately got to know everyone in the area, all the tour operators and taxi drivers, any flower shop or salon or tobacconist. I became an expert at obtaining what small "contraband" the rigors of spa diet prohibited, and made myself a fair amount of money in the process.

It was always about making people happy. And I was good at it.

The season was over in November, and in spite of a very well-rehearsed and heated argument against it, once more I had to go home and help my father. He had a new restaurant in Nördlingen, an even bigger place called Das Deutsche Haus, where he worked himself, and us, harder than ever. I was beginning to think Mutti planned her illnesses for the season, so they could use my extra hands.

Chacha left for her hometown, Basse, in Germany. She would stay there with family and friends until we decided what the next step might be. I hated to see her go, and I hated to leave behind our good times in Bad Pyrmont.

December 20, 1957 was my twenty-first birthday. The family completely forgot. We worked all day as usual, and I kept waiting for the party to start. Every time I heard a glass clink, every time a new customer whooshed in the door behind a burst of cold air, or the loud laughter of a particularly jovial table would catch my attention, I thought *now*. Now the singing will start. Now Mutti will bring one of her incredible cakes out of the kitchen. Now my family will celebrate me.

But nothing happened. Nothing except dirty plates and empty glasses, and talk of Christmas on the way and more busy days ahead. I went to bed in a black mood.

The next morning, I was flipping chairs over, taking them off the tables so we could set up for lunch.

"What are you doing?" asked my father.

"Setting up," I said, and flipped another chair down off the table. Mutti came out to say good morning. She looked tired, but she smiled at us around the room, and asked if anyone wanted something to eat.

"No," I said.

She walked up to me, reading me as usual, between the lines. My face told her something that my voice never did at those times. I couldn't hide feelings from her, not since I was a small boy.

"What's the matter, Adi?"

"Nothing." I slammed the last chair onto the floor and it made my father bark some scolding. "But, oh," I said, "*thank you*. Thank you for remembering my twenty-first birthday last night. I really appreciate all the presents and the nice party. It was just great, and I can't thank you enough."

Mutti was shocked. So was I. I couldn't believe I spoke like that, especially to her, especially knowing she wasn't well. We stood in the empty restaurant and waited for somebody to say something. I felt my righteous indignation souring into childishness. And for the first time I felt cheated, cheated out of festivities and childish things, by hard work and a difficult world. But no amount of sarcasm, or blame or indignation was going to get that back for me.

Vati poured us all a cup of coffee. Then he added a touch of brandy from one of the better bottles on the top shelf. We clinked our cups and said "Prost," then quietly drank together. There was nothing to say. Growing up, I suppose, is like that for some people. Quiet. Without a lot of fuss. After my parents went back to work, I sat a while with my coffee and decided what I had to do for myself.

Adi (left), Falk Volkhardt (owner of the Bayerischer Hof) and Chacha (third from left, with heart) celebrating Oktoberfest with friends

CHAPTER 15

Munich

I think that morning helped my father finally accept that I was not going to follow in the family business, and this was the last time I'd be available as temporary help. Something in me was my own, and he could see it. Besides I was in love, with my career as well as my future wife. I went back to work somewhat more a man than a boy.

In the spring, Chacha and I both managed to get jobs in Munich. I was to be Front Desk Clerk at the Bayerischer Hof, and she had a position at the Vier Jahreszeiten. She moved into an apartment with a girlfriend on Wilhelm Leuschner Strasse and I boarded with a family on the same street, Mr. & Mrs. Horst Blaik.

Life in Munich was about having fun. For the first time I had the money and the time to spend in the company of people my own age, to enjoy being young, and to occasionally be the customer in somebody else's restaurant for a change. Chacha and I made friends with other hotel workers like Nik Klotz and Dieter Mayring, and we did everything together. Dieter's father had a small hotel with a very nice restaurant and bar in Schwabing, a wonderful place where all the artists would go. We ended up most of our nights there, even after the late shifts.

During one of our nights at Mayring's, we realized we all had the next day off. This was such a rare thing that we decided to celebrate with a trip to the Autobahn See and a picnic lunch. The Autobahn See was the creation of good German engineering. When they built the highway called the Autobahn they needed a lot of earth to fill and level the road. They dug out a huge hole, filled it with water, and called it the Autobahn See.

Dieter borrowed his father's car and we packed up our swimsuits, a picnic lunch and some beers, and headed out to the lake. The men were swimming races and showing off for the ladies, who mostly sat on the stone wall, dangling their toes in the water and chatting about whatever ladies chat about. After a while, but before I'd had a drop to drink, seven or eight of us decided to climb up on the wall and all dive in at the same time. It would be a terrific stunt, guaranteed to impress the girls.

"You're crazy," said Chacha. "You'll break your neck."

I laughed her off. After my conquest of the Kessel and the Danube, this was nothing. I joined the rest of the guys in my position at the end of the line. The water level was about four feet below the wall, and we made a big show of getting ready, in our best Johnny Weismuller poses. Everyone was laughing as Dieter called out, "One, two, three…Go!"

I hit bottom like an anchor tied to a cement block.

The water, at my end of the wall, was way too shallow for diving. For a second I couldn't figure out what had happened. Then I thought my arms were stuck in the mud. But instead of drowning, I freed myself without too much trouble and swam back to the rest of the group. I must have looked strange when I got out of the water; blood was running down my face. Chacha said, "You have rocks in your head."

"I do not," I said. "I told you there was nothing to worry about."

"No," she said. "Real rocks. In your hair. Look."

My scalp was full of little pebbles from the lake floor.

"What happened?" she asked.

I told her, not without embarrassment, that I'd hit bottom when we all dove in.

"You're going to the hospital for an X-ray," she said. And that was that.

Reluctantly, I left the party and she and Dieter took me to the hospital. After some tests and X-rays of my head, it was decided that I did not have a concussion or any other reason to be concerned.

"I told you I was all right," I said to Chacha. "I don't even have a headache."

"If you try a stunt like that again, you will," said Chacha. "If I have to give it to you myself."

I decided that diving was possibly not my sport. None of them let me forget it.

One day Nik Klotz came home with an idea to help defend my male ego. "I have the perfect plan for you Adi," he said. "For all three of us." Dieter and I just sat and listened. Nik always had the perfect plan for something. "Seriously, " he said. "You want to learn how to fight, right?"

I was always a skinny kid, even at twenty-two. And I grew up in an unfavorable time for skinny kids, with the world determined, it seemed, to push me around forever if it couldn't actually kill me. I got beat up more than once in *Hotelfachschule,* for being a Knapsack German instead of a Bavarian, for being the captain of the banquet team when I was not even eighteen. Mostly I got beat up because there was always somebody who could, and who thought they had a good reason. "I want to learn how to defend myself," I said. "That is a whole different thing."

"Exactly right," said Nik. "Well, listen to this. I just heard that Siegi Klauenbrunner is here in Munich."

"He is? The Bavarian Lightweight Champ? What's he doing here?"

"He's opened a gymnasium, and he's taking on new students. You want to be a fighter. He's the best coach in the country."

"We can't afford it."

"Of course we can. We'll find a way. And if all three of us sign up together, he's got to give us a discount. Come on. What's worse? Being a little more broke than you already are, or letting some *Arschloch* beat you up for the rest of your life?"

I had to agree with him. By the end of the week, the three of us were apprentice boxers, and our coach was as good as his reputation. He was tough. But I was the product of Vati, the war, Catholic

School, the bottom of the Danube, Pepo Brehm and Herr Karpf, so I wasn't easily discouraged. I was only about 160 pounds and still growing taller, so he started every workout with the barbells and the medicine ball. I would pump and sweat till my arms and chest were aching, and then he'd make me run before I put on boxing gloves. Coach was very careful to teach us the proper technique before we were ever allowed to hit anything alive. First he had us shadow box, then practice on the speed bag or the heavy bag while he shouted instructions.

It was almost a year before he let us put on the big 16-ounce gloves and spar a little bit in three-round matches. He didn't allow us to actually punch each other, only just touch our gloves to target spots. We were starting to feel powerful, dying to try our skills with an opponent. For me, all those hours with the barbells were making a difference when I flexed in the mirror, but I had only the beginning sense of my own strength. I couldn't wait to feel a real punch connect with something, or someone.

One night we had decided to meet at Mayring's place after work, and I walked along Ludwigstrasse by myself, checking out a pretty girl here and there. I saw the steep stone staircase leading up to the front door of the bar, and thought about how sometimes it was a lot easier walking up those stairs than coming back down.

As I crossed Ludwigstrasse, I passed an older woman walking in the opposite direction. She carried a cane and had a scarf over her head, peasant style. I heard a wolf whistle, and from the corner of my eye I saw two guys leaning on the corner lamppost. They harassed the old lady as she got closer, making fun of her walk and saying rude things. She tried to pass them by, but one pulled up the back of her skirt and waggled his tongue. The others laughed raucously.

"Hey," I called out. "What are you trying to do? Leave her alone." They yelled something back in my direction, but I didn't approach them, just stood and watched. One of them muttered something under his breath. They let her go. I waited a moment longer, feeling like I'd done a good deed, then turned and started up the stairs.

Halfway up I felt a hard tug on my shoulder. The guy whipped me around in a rage. "Who do you think you are?" he said. I called him an *Arschloch* and he screamed into my face "You take that back!"

I didn't think. I didn't hesitate. I cocked back my right hand and fired it square into his face. His nose collapsed. His eyes went blank.

I saw him start to go backward and I grabbed at him to punch his face again, but his shirt slipped through my fingers and he fell. I watched him float, arms flailing for a long time, until his head hit the sidewalk with an inhuman sound. I stood there, my right still clenched. He did not move.

Dieter ran out. "Oh God," he said. "You killed him!"

We didn't know what to do. The other guys had disappeared, but people were starting to come out of the bar. I thought the police were on the way. A million things flashed through my mind. I thought about prison, about the Czech policeman and the revolver in the desk drawer. I wanted to run but my feet were frozen to the step. He's dead, I thought. I killed him. I should never have hit him so hard. I should never have hit him. I should never have learned how to hit him. I should never have wanted to learn. I thought I heard sirens. I heard the Devil coming down the street with the war, and the rumbling Mongols on the little horses. I was back on the river bottom with the whirlpool sucking me down and no way to get back up and breathe.

Then he opened his eyes.

Dieter had run back to the bar and brought his father out. Herr Mayring had a car and helped us get him to the hospital. His head was fractured, he had a broken nose and a few less teeth, but he would recover. The doctor didn't see any need for the police, and so we left.

I took a long walk. I walked for the rest of the night. I can't say I exactly prayed, but I did make a promise to myself and whoever else might be listening that I would never hit anyone again in my life. It was as if all the violence I'd grown up with was compressed into that one punch. I didn't want to learn anything else about fighting. I knew enough about it for a lifetime.

A few weeks later I ran into the guy at almost the same place on Ludwigstrasse. I braced myself for trouble, but I kept my hands in my pockets. What he did caught me completely off guard.

"Thank you," he said.

I didn't understand.

"For taking me to the hospital and making sure I was okay." He was embarrassed, but had made up his mind what he wanted to tell me. I wondered how long had been waiting for me to pass by. "I learned a lesson that night," he said. "And you shouldn't feel bad about it." He shook my hand and left. I never saw him again.

Place de la Concorde

CHAPTER 16

Paris

Falk Volkhardt was my second mentor, after Viktor Singer. He was the owner of the Hotel Bayerischer Hof, where I worked, and had great plans to open Munich's first major nightclub. He knew of my background, and wanted me to manage the place when it opened. "What do you think, Köhler?" he asked.

"Mr. Volkhardt," I said, "my dream is to work my way up at the Front Desk. I want to be the Manager of a great hotel one day. And I've already learned the restaurant business inside and out."

"Yes you have," he said. "But a Hotel Manager has to have a tremendous amount of experience. He has to speak languages, and know how to deal with all kinds of people in every kind of situation. It's not something one can do overnight," he said. "And the nightclub is a great opportunity for a young man. I wouldn't offer it to just anybody."

"Yes sir," I said. "But, what if…" I took a breath. "What if, in five years, I learned two languages. Would you hire me back?"

There was a long pause. Finally, he said, "Köhler, that's what we're going to do." He shook my hand. We had a deal.

I decided to learn French first, and remembering Viktor Singer's advice to only work at first class hotels, I researched the best properties in Paris. I sent letters to all of them, the Ritz, the Georges V, the Meurice, and Hôtel de Crillon, owned by the famous champagne family, Taittinger. It was my good luck to end up there, as *Stagière*

Comptabilité (bookkeeper) for the front desk operation in October of 1961.

The Hôtel de Crillon had been a Paris landmark since it was commissioned as a palace by Louis XV in 1758. It was transformed into a luxury residential hotel in 1909 and welcomed royalty, international celebrities and politicians into its ninety-five rooms and fifty-two "Grand Apartments." Located in the heart of the city, it was close to the fancy shopping district of Faubourg St.-Honoré, and in walking distance of the Champs Elysées, the Louvre and many other famous places.

I found a room to rent from a Monsieur and Madame Bernard Flé on Rue Boisy D'Anglase. Madame spoke very good German because she was born in Alsace-Lorraine. She married a Frenchman and moved to Paris where she ran their bed and breakfast. Monsieur only spoke French, but they were very, very good to me, and especially Madame was a tremendous help in making Paris my new, or next, home. I had heard about the City of Light all my life, but I'd never set foot inside France. All I knew about it was from pre-war history books, slivers of bad news during the war, and post-war stories of glamour, romance and *haute couture*. I once again found myself in a place I had never been. Some of my friends thought I was out of my mind. I thought I was lucky beyond belief.

The only French I knew was on a menu, so I had to learn fast. You couldn't get very far in Paris by only saying "Cabernet Sauvignon." Immediately, I applied to Alliance Française, a special language school that taught French to foreigners. The beginner's class was 8:00 a.m. to 12:00 noon every day, and after that I worked 4:00 to 11:00 p.m. six days a week.

Later, I met a German named Helmut Hoermann (who later became president of Hilton Hotels), and we became good friends. We decided to share an apartment, which we found on the fourth floor of an old building. The rent was 800 *nouveaux Francs* (about forty dollars), and we had some great times there.

After about a year, the Hôtel was pleased with how fast I had learned to speak French. They made me the very first non-French *Deuxième Cashier,* a prestigious and trusted position in the Front.

My main job was to exchange currency, and I was responsible to handle millions of francs every day. In those days, the hotel made a ten-percent commission on any exchange, and the Cashier was tipped on top of that.

This promotion inspired me to throw a party in our apartment. Helmut was nervous about the idea, but I said, "Leave everything to me." We were both anxious to impress our French colleagues, and show them that we weren't all German pigs. Unfortunately, I didn't have much money to work with, but I did have a master plan.

I spent weeks rifling through the empties at the Hôtel de Crillon, gathering up all the best wine bottles I could find. I took them home at the end of my shift and cleaned them up. When I had enough collected, I went to the wine market and bought the cheapest red wine I could find, filled the good bottles with it, and replaced the corks.

It was great. Everyone praised the wine and toasted us like true connoisseurs, congratulating us on our excellent tastes and kissing their fingers like we did when we were kids. We got ten or fifteen people pleasantly drunk and one of the guys, Paul, stood up and asked the question for everybody.

"Monsieur Köhler," he began, wavering a little on his feet. I listened carefully. *"Vous n'êtes pas comme les autres 'salles boches.' Pourquoi-pas?"* (You are not like the others, meaning other "dirty pig" Germans. Why not?)

I cleared my throat. The wine was very helpful in improving my accent, if not my grammar. *"Mes amis,"* I began. "There are three reasons why I came to Paris. First, to learn the French language. Second, to try some of your beautiful French wines. And last but not least, if I'm lucky enough, to make love to some of your beautiful French women." This drew lots of "ooooo's" and a round of applause. "I did not come to Paris to goose-step up and down the Champs Elysées."

It slayed them. Paul kissed me on both cheeks. Helmut turned purple. We never told them about the wine.

Good times notwithstanding, I missed Chacha. On somewhat of an impulse, I called her up and asked her to marry me. She said "Yes, when?" I told her I would have to check with my boss, who unfortunately would not bend the schedule, even for a wedding. So I left on an afternoon train, and three days later came back to work a married man.

We got married twice, actually, which was the custom. Once at a small civil ceremony at the courthouse and once in the Lutheran Church in Basse. It was January 9, 1962, and when I looked at my beautiful, glowing bride I remembered my mother saying how I would be lucky in life. She was right. She almost always was.

So I changed her first name and her last name too. I hope Mrs. Kohler will forgive me for not remembering the first moment I saw her. But there was never any one specific thing that drew me to her, and no gong sounded in my heart that told me I would marry this woman. Rather what I remember was a gradual growing to know the beautiful lady on the inside of the one on the outside. This was and is a woman of endless energy, iron will, courageous fire in a crisis, or when one of her causes is up against the wall.

We grew up in similar circumstances, children of the war, and as we grow older together now, I know that the steel in her was forged during those early years. And the fun we've had together, the adventures, well, I can take a little of the credit for that. As for the teamwork it takes to run great hotels and raise a happy family at the same time, I give her full credit for that, something I'm sure I've never acknowledged nearly enough. All I can say is when I count my many blessings, I start and end with her.

CHAPTER 17

The Wild West

After two years in Paris, I felt pretty comfortable speaking French and decided to start learning my next language. I had promised to Falk Volkhardt I'd learn two languages in five years and return to Bayerischer Hof. I chose English, and sent applications to several good hotels in London. In July 1963, I got an offer from Claridge's that was exactly what I was looking for. Chacha and I were very excited.

Before I had a chance to accept, I got another letter. This one from an old friend, Peter Singer (no relation to Viktor), with a different kind of offer. Peter and I had worked together at Bayerischer Hof before he moved to the United States. His goal was the same as mine, learn languages and go back to the hotels in Europe, but something had changed. Peter said he was opening a German restaurant, Peter's Hofbrau, in Scottsdale, Arizona, and would I be available to help?

Arizona. Cowboys. American money and a chance to get rich. I'd already decided to leave Paris. They spoke English in America; I could still learn the language and come back. But the restaurant business again? I'd promised myself I'd never go back. Still, the idea was so tempting. Chacha and I talked it over; we decided I should go ahead first and get established. I started on the paperwork, typing visa requests and travel papers and carrying them from office to office.

Along the way I lost my umlaut. French typewriters didn't have one; so even though I'd typed the forms on a good German machine, my passport and my green card were without. By the time I got to

America, I was Adi Kohler with an ordinary "o." For years I never noticed.

We arrived at 9:00 at night; it was the middle of July. Like all proper European travelers I was wearing my good suit, long-sleeved shirt and tie. It was a hundred degrees on the ground. I thought I had landed in Hell.

Peter picked me up at the airport and we drove into Scottsdale where he had a little apartment. The next day we went to see the restaurant. I was shocked. The place was a mess; the pantry was empty; the kitchen equipment didn't work. It was a long, long way from being ready for business. He promised me that everything would be in great shape by October. All I could think was, "What the hell am I going to do between now and October?" I was just about flat broke. If you want to ruin a friendship, open a restaurant together.

I immediately did what my family had always done, the best with what I had. I walked to the first restaurant on the street and, using every English word I knew, I asked for a job. The next day I was flipping burgers in a place called the Red Balloon. In spite of the fact that hamburgers are supposed to come from Hamburg, up until then I had never eaten one in my life. And I promised myself if I ever got out of there, I would never eat one again. It was not a taste I culti-vated, and neither was the all-too-familiar smell of greasy kitchen and the hard work that went along with that. At night, I was back at Peter's Hofbrau, cleaning and scrubbing, trying to get things orga-nized. I was back in the restaurant business again, knee-deep in it.

Nik Klotz flew in from Bermuda to help get the restaurant open, and Chacha came from Germany on December 19, in time for my birthday. Having her around made everything better, but even she couldn't help Peter's Hofbrau. It was one disaster after another. On the second of January 1964, we had had enough. A friend with a car helped us move our few things out of the apartment and I slid the key under the door.

Nik helped me get a job and a room in the Casablanca Inn, a small hotel right there in Scottsdale. Chacha was doing incredibly well with her English in such a short time, and started work as a telephone operator. Because we needed the money, and because of my training, they asked me to take on the position of Sommelier (wine steward) too. So I worked Room Service from 6:00-10:00 a.m. and then served wine for lunch and dinner until we closed at 10:00 p.m.

In spite of the long hours, we found time to be happy in Arizona. When I could get away from work, I was able to be with horses again. Once I got some money in my pocket, one of the first things I did was buy myself a pair of blue jeans and a cowboy hat. I wanted to fit in in this country, and if that meant being a cowboy, well, I might not be able to sound like an American right away, but there was no reason not to look the part. I went out to one of the ranches and rented a western saddle and a good trail horse. I took my time with him, the same way I had done with the Belgians. I spoke low and gentle, asking him to help me out so we could take a ride. He didn't seem to mind my limited English, and it didn't take long before we were ranging through some beautiful country just like in the cowboy movies.

I decided Arizona was not Hell after all, just a really, really warm Heaven.

Those long afternoons in the saddle were more or less the middle of a long trail which began back in my walking cowboy days on Herr Mayer's farm, and lead into my joining the Rancheros Visitadores, perhaps the most prestigious Western riding club in the country. My good friend Ray Corliss introduced me to this interesting group of horsemen in May in 1989, when hundreds of Rancheros, seventeen entire camps of them, gathered in the Santa Ynez Valley in California for a week's worth of a completely different life. This is not a half-fantasy macho "City Slicker" experience. This is a taste of real cowboying: calf-branding, cannoneering, cattle cutting, horse races and horse shows, roping and trap shooting, and the great Western custom of

On the trail with El Campo de Los Bustardos, Rancheros Visitadores

having a real good time. The roster is strictly classified, and I might be subject to branding or worse if I revealed any names. However, I can say that I'm proud to be listed among El Campo De Los Bustardos, along with former presidents, five-star generals, and horse and cattle ranching elite from all over the country.

As a matter of fact, it was on that ride in 1989 where I smoked my first cigar. I was sitting on one of my favorite quarterhorses as we rambled across the countryside, taking in the scenery, and relaxing to the rhythm of the saddle, as I'd done when I was a kid. My mind was off on its own.

A friend of mine rode up. "Kohler," he said. "You look like you're bored to death." He held up one of his Cubanos, cut the end off and lit it for me. "Here," he said. "Try this." He passed it over and I savored that big fat Cuban cigar for two of the most relaxing hours I can remember. The horse even seemed to enjoy it.

Being with the Rancheros is a completely different experience for me. On the Ride I don't have to be the boss. I don't have to account for my time or make any decisions. The Rancheros take you as you are. They don't ask a lot of questions. And they have the good common sense to know the difference between when a man wants to talk, and when he wants to be left alone. It's a week's worth of camaraderie, open spaces, good food, great music, a little drinking and a lot of laughing. Or is it vice versa?

I did have a horse of my own for a while, a great Appaloosa officially named "Sundown Chief," but I called him Brother. He was a hell of a horse, and good company after a difficult day. He would listen to me go and on about the guests or the meetings or the myriad of things that got under my skin. And he never once told me to shut up.

I stopped riding Brother when he was thirty-two years old, and he decided to retire and take it easy. When he was thirty-five, time just caught up with him, and he had trouble staying on his feet. I called my then and present friend Dr. Charlie Campbell, who came over to the stables right away. The three of us talked it over.

Rationally, I understood the decision to put an animal down. I had assisted Herr Doktor Karl Niklasch in ending their miseries many times. Even so, when the time comes to say goodbye, it is not an easy thing. When they look at you, especially when a horse looks at you with those great round eyes, you see something indescribable. It is not fear of death, although I'm sure they know, or anger towards you for causing it. It is something like forgiveness. As if in their last few minutes of life, they would reach out and send comfort to you.

I held Brother's head in my arms until he fell asleep.

He's grazing in greener pastures now.

In Scottsdale, the end of April was the end of the season and we needed to look for other jobs or move on. The Casablanca's GM, Royal Treadway, suggested I try for a seasonal job at one of the Rockefeller properties in the Grand Tetons National Park in Wyoming. He arranged an interview with Richard Erb in their Human Resources department, and Chacha and I were both offered jobs at Jackson Lake Lodge.

We bought our very first car: a 1957 Chevy station wagon, red and white. She was a beauty and we named her "Dicke Berta" (Big Bertha). We loaded her up and headed out on our first great American road trip. I had never driven so far or stopped for gas so many times. Dicke was a big car, and she was hungry all the time. In the four-day trip to Wyoming, other than a stop at the Grand Canyon, most of our sightseeing was gas stations. When we finally reached Wyoming, we were completely exhausted and completely broke. At least we'd have a bed to sleep in when we got there, and most likely something to eat in the cafeteria.

We arrived in the early afternoon, to one of the most beautiful places I had ever seen, like the storybook paintings on the walls of my father's restaurant. A forested retreat, Jackson Lake Lodge sat on a serene plateau, with fifty-foot windows looking over the Grand Tetons mountain range. The air was so clear and bright I thought I might be looking at brand new colors, just invented for the place.

Inside, the front desk clerk had been expecting us. While we were registering, she said, "Oh, by the way Mr. Kohler, there's an envelope here for you."

"An envelope?" I asked. Immediately I started to worry. Oh no, is Peter looking for us? Is there trouble at home? Are we being deported?

"Yes," she said. She pulled it out of a pigeonhole. "Look, it's from the government."

I had never seen an envelope from the United States Government before, but I was sure it was bad. "All these years," I said to Chacha in German, "I stayed out of the German army, and now I'm being drafted by the Americans."

The desk clerk looked at us curiously. "Is something wrong?"

If my hands were not shaking, they were at least fumbling with the envelope. I took a breath and ripped it opened. It was a check for $375.

"Was is das?" I asked the desk clerk. She was staring at me.

"Well, it's a tax refund," she said. "From your last job. You get those in April. Every year."

We laughed like crazy people. Then we cleaned up and drove into the town of Jackson Hole, where we treated ourselves to the biggest steak dinner and the best bottle of red wine on the menu. It was the start of a great season.

That summer in Wyoming I realized I left my umlaut in Paris. I was at a get-together with the rest of the hotel staff, and Jim Reed came up and asked, "What the hell is your last name?"

"Köhler," I told him, with the umlaut, which of course wasn't on my nametag.

"What?" he said, "Curler?"

"No, Köhler," I tried again, with my very best accent.

"Huh?" Jim tried to pronounce it properly. "Cooler? Keeler?" He just couldn't get his tongue around it.

"Well it's Köhler," I said. "Because of the umlaut."

"The what? I don't see any umlaut."

I thought he was kidding, but I'd play along. I whipped out my wallet. "Look here," I said. "My identification papers. See? Right there." I held up my Green Card with authority.

"Where?"

To my utter astonishment, my umlaut was missing. My name had changed and I didn't even know it.

Jim laughed like crazy at the look on my face. He slapped me on the shoulder. "You're Adi Kohler now, pal," he said. "Welcome to America."

That was the summer I met Mr. and Mrs. Laurance S. Rockefeller, as we were getting ready to close for the winter. Although we did little more than shake hands, I was very impressed with how he interacted with the staff. Neither arrogant or overbearing, he expressed a genuine and generous appreciation for our work. He was a true gentleman, and I thought this is the kind of man who understands what it is to be first class. I wanted to keep working for him.

We needed to find somewhere to work for the winter. Mr. Rockefeller's properties in the U.S. Virgin Islands and Puerto Rico were open and busy all year round. Chacha and I had plans to start a family, and for that we needed to settle down in a place where I could work year-round and make a good salary. I put in a request and the company recommended me to Bill Faber, the General Manager at Caneel Bay Plantation on the Island of St. John. I had never even heard of the *Jungfrauen Inseln,* but the Virgin Islands sounded like the perfect place. Not long after my conversation with Bill, the offer came through.

Chacha and I planned our second road trip. We'd drive across the country from Wyoming to Miami, then fly the rest of the way. We loaded up the car and headed east. Unfortunately, Dicke Berta had other plans, and in St. Louis she started having engine trouble. We took her to a mechanic, but the repairs were much too expensive. He offered us $375 and we decided to leave her behind. As I took the suitcases out of the car, I remembered Doktor Niklasch, the veterinarian. I explained the situation to Dicke Berta and patted her on the fender as we left.

We flew southward in stages, from St. Louis to Miami, San Juan and St. Thomas. With every stop, the weather got hotter and muggier, the airport got older and the plane got smaller. The last flight was aboard a little propeller plane, with no air-conditioning and all the windows open. When we sat down, they put a board into the aisle so nobody could leave their seat. Someone in the back had a cage of fighting chickens that squawked bloody murder when we landed.

The St. Thomas airport was one big barn, noisy, dusty, and full of brightly-clothed people milling around or crowded into tiny bars for one last rum and Coke before their flight. A tall Black man, shiny-skinned with very white teeth found us in the crowd, searching for Baggage Claim.

"Good day, Sir," he said.

"Hello, I'm Adi Kohler," I said and offered my hand. He shook it hard.

"Welcome to St. Thomas, Sir. Mum."

He had a funny accent, but we understood that our luggage didn't arrive on the plane with us. In fact it most likely wouldn't be sent until later that evening, or maybe tomorrow, but they'd have it sent to the hotel. He pointed us to the "taxi bus" that took us to the National Park docks, and from there a boat would ferry us to Caneel Bay. We went where he told us to go. The humid air was so heavy it felt more like swimming than walking. Mosquitoes buzzed around our ankles.

Finally on the boat, crossing the channel between St. Thomas and St. John, I felt like I could breathe again. With the evening sea breeze in my face, I watched water the color of Arizona's best turquoise blend into pinks and purples of tropical sunset that looked like it was painted with fire. And as we approached the dock at Caneel, I saw the torches flicker over a pair of perfect white beaches, hinting at a secret hideaway nestled in the crooks between rows of rolling green hills.

I'll never forget. It was one of those sights that makes everyone a poet.

CHAPTER 18

Beach Life

Caneel Bay Plantation was arrayed along a little peninsula between the Carribbean Sea and the Atlantic Ocean, amid acres and acres of manicured lawns, mango trees, coconut palms and rolling green hills. It had seven picturebook white-sand beaches each with their own name and character: Honeymoon, Caneel, Little Caneel, Scott Beach, Turtle Bay, Hawk's Nest and Paradise, and each with a cluster of discreetly-built, low-rise guestrooms around it. It was an abandoned sugar cane farm that Laurance S. Rockefeller found in 1952, when the population of St. John was only 400 people. He had an idea for a luxury retreat and bought the place. The next year he built the infrastructure to support his dream, including roads, utilities and a water desalinization plant. He purchased the surrounding 5,000 acres of land which he then donated to the government to become the U.S. Virgin Islands National Park, thus guaranteeing the privacy and unspoiled nature of Caneel.

There were no televisions in the rooms, no telephones and no room keys in order to give the guests as much of a natural luxury experience as possible. Providing this "natural" experience was a lot of work. Caneel was such a big place that right away Bill Faber taught me a concept people now call MBWA, "Management By Walking Around." I moved from one end of the property to the other, stopping to touch base in every area, the dining rooms, the kitchens, the front desk, shops, back of the house. I made a tour almost every day, and tried to put my feet in the guests' shoes. I made mental notes of

123

what needed repair and I made an effort to speak to everyone I passed, and call them by name.

One afternoon, I was walking by the guest rooms along Scott Beach and I heard a noise from one of the linen rooms. I opened the door and surprised a couple deeply engaged in a non-work activity.

"What are you doing?" I said.

Without missing a beat, the man said, "Making babies, Sir!"

I closed the door. I was furious, but something made me stop and think before I did another thing. For the briefest second I remembered Mr. Karpf, purple-faced and screaming at some stupid mistake I'd made. I said to myself, "Everybody's entitled to one. Kohler you're new here. You don't know these people and you don't know who they might be married to or what the situation is."

In a few minutes they came out, embarrassed and scared to death as they finished buttoning clothes. I wanted to laugh, but I gave them the stern look of the new boss. "Obviously this is not where you're supposed to be."

"Very sorry sir," said the woman. They both hung their heads. They had on uniforms for different departments. The man held his hat in his large hands.

"Look," I said. "Both of you have work to do, and this is not what you do on the job. Now go back to where you are supposed to be and nobody has to know anything about this." They looked at each other, not sure what to think. "Get moving," I said. "But don't ever do anything like this again."

A lot of managers would have handled it differently I'm sure, but these two people became two of my better employees. I had minded my own business and treated them like human beings, and they treated me with respect afterward. I still had a lot to learn about our new home, but I had made a decent start with some of the people.

In October 1964, we found out Mr. Rockefeller was developing two additional resorts which were to open in early 1965. One was Little Dix Bay on Virgin Gorda in the British Virgin Islands, and the other was Mauna Kea Beach Hotel on the Island of Hawai'i. To do this, his advisors suggested that LSR form his own hotel management group, with Richard Holtzmann as president. The new company would be called Rockresorts Inc., and would include the three Wyoming properties, the Woodstock Inn, Dorado Beach in Puerto Rico, Caneel Bay, Little Dix Bay and Mauna Kea.

When Dick and his family came to visit Caneel, I was standing on the dock to greet them and escort them to their room. He immediately impressed me as one of the most personable, caring and intelligent gentlemen I've ever had the pleasure to meet. I knew Mr. Rockefeller had found a great hotel man to run his new company.

Laurance and Mary Rockefeller visited two or three times a year, and always stayed in Cottage #7. I was able to get to know LSR better during those visits, and I often wondered how it could happen that two people from such completely different worlds could sit in the same room and speak the same language, much less share the same hopes and ideas for our hotel. I wondered if I had been born with his resources, and he had been born a *Rucksack Bayer,* would we have managed to end up in the same place? I was always aware of how lucky I was to end up working for him.

October 16, 1965 was another lucky day, when Ulrike Katharina Kohler was born. Because there was no hospital on St. John, Chacha had gone to Puerto Rico several weeks earlier, and I flew over to bring them home. Fatherhood was something I had always wanted, but I'm not sure anyone is ever quite prepared for the experience. I was awestruck by her from the moment I first saw her. When the amazement wore off a little bit (It never does completely!) I couldn't imagine my life before she came along.

She was tiny but always full of energy, and such a busy little thing that we right away nicknamed her Bienchen (little bee). Her "real" name had been very carefully selected by her mother and myself, during many hours of conversation. We named her Ulrike (ool-ree-kay) because we both loved it, and Katharina after Chacha's mother. Well, nobody could pronounce her name. They called her "Ricky" and stumbled over the word, so we started calling her Bieni (beenie) and it stuck.

We were very fortunate to know a wonderful local woman named Kathleen Williams from the island of Nevis. She became part of our family and helped Chacha raise Bieni with a kind and loving spirit that I'm sure rubbed off on our daughter. We moved into the manager's house that overlooked the tennis courts and for the next three years Bieni grew up with wild donkeys in her backyard, seven beaches to romp on, and visiting playmates from all over the world.

In 1967, the company advised that the best way for me to advance was to get experience with broader resorts, those with bigger food & beverage operations, golf courses and casinos. I decided to transfer to another of Mr. Rockefeller's hotels, Dorado Beach in Puerto Rico, without ever visiting the place. We went from genteel, European spa-style Caneel Bay with only 166 rooms, to Dorado, a 310-room hotel and casino with a world-class golf course, right outside the capitol city of San Juan, decidedly Latin. It was quite a change.

Rockresorts had plans to add a second property, the Cerromar Beach Hotel, as a sister to Dorado. The two would operate in concert like a mega-resort, with unlimited possibilities for success in the future. We worked harder than ever, but it was an exciting time to be involved, and we had an excellent team that was up to the challenge.

We were extremely fortunate to have two outstanding teaching professionals in Nick Bolletieri at the tennis courts, and Chi Chi Rodriguez on the golf course. Chi Chi was originally from Puerto Rico, and came back to Dorado after making a name for himself on the tour. His wife Evalani was from Waianae, Hawai'i and she invited Chacha and me to our very first *lu'au*. It was an incredible affair for which she had brought in not only special food like *poi* and *sashimi* (raw fish), but *lei,* music, *hula* dancers and enough aloha to go around the island twice.

Chi Chi talked me into learning golf because he said it would help my career. He taught me to play, and gave me my first set of clubs in a custom-made green and white golf bag inscribed "to Adi from Chi Chi," which had a permanent corner in my office. However, golf takes a long time to play and my busy schedule didn't permit the hours away from the office. Tennis was faster. Nick gave me my first tennis lesson and taught me that to enjoy the game was the most important thing. I applied that lesson to golf, too.

Shortly after arriving at Dorado, I got involved with an organization called the Confrérie de la Chaîne des Rôtisseurs (roughly "the brotherhood linked by the rotisserie"). This is a five hundred-year-old epicurean society with exacting standards and notable membership worldwide. Jim Cimino was the first Bailli (president) in Puerto Rico and he hosted one of his first dinners at our hotel.

We had never done anything like this before. Emilio Perez, our F&B Director, and I worked like crazy to produce a five-star dinner that the high-minded society gourmets would never forget. We took the chefs to the marketplace for the best local produce and fish, and what we couldn't find we flew in from the mainland. We challenged them to create a menu that put their entire staff to the test, and promised to back it up with perfect service. We hand-picked the waiters and trained them on the side between their regular shifts. We had the best florist on the island make masterpieces for the tables, and found a band from Santurce, guaranteed to make everyone dance, no matter how much they had to eat.

I myself was lighting the last candle when the Maitre d' opened the ballroom doors. As the guests came in, I saw on their faces the look I must have had so long ago when Viktor Singer saw me admiring the View Jahreszeiten for the first time. This is what we are supposed to do, I thought as I snuffed out the match. No more stealing red wine bottles. This is the real thing.

We blew them away. A couple of weeks later, I received an engraved invitation to join the Confrérie. If I didn't send it to Viktor, I intended to.

On November 14, 1968, our family was blessed with a son. He was born in the same hospital in San Juan where Chacha had Bieni. Because I was working as usual, some friends saw him first, and when they told me I had a son, I couldn't believe it. I thought I was the luckiest man alive. We named him Christian Adolf, passing the name from me to him, which was also my father's and grandfather's.

Life was now even busier, and we were very fortunate to find a wonderful woman to help Chacha raise our children. Ely Martinez was a gem, and a permanent auntie to Christian and Bieni. She joined our household when she was eighteen, and was the perfect addition to our growing family.

Puerto Rico was a very interesting place, and people had a particularly interesting way of doing things. One afternoon a gentleman dressed like a priest came to our house, and introduced himself as Walter Kurz. He was the former Bishop in China and on his return to the U.S. Mainland, was sent to Puerto Rico for a vacation. He asked if he could talk to me on a personal matter.

He told me that some Catholic friends in town mentioned they heard the Assistant General Manager at Dorado was a non-practicing Catholic who had not had a Catholic wedding. He asked in all seriousness if we wouldn't like to be married in the faith with two Catholic witnesses, so we didn't have to continue living in sin.

Now Chacha and I had already been married twice in Germany, first in the government office, then in the Protestant church in Basse. But Bishop Kurz was so sincere that I said I would talk to Chacha.

"What?" she said.

"Well apparently there's some talk that we never had a proper wedding."

"What concern is that of anyone's?"

"Do you mean you wouldn't marry me again? Even if I asked very nicely?"

She smiled. "Well how would we do it?"

"Apparently this Bishop Kurz has to get a special exemption from the Pope. But he's offered to take care of everything, and it seems to be very important to the Catholic Church, and our immortal souls as well."

"Well I don't know about all that," she said. "But as long as I don't have to promise to convert, or to commit the children to being Catholics, then I don't have a problem with it."

"Thank you," I said. "I would hate to have to marry someone else." I think she hit me then, but we laughed.

The wedding was great fun. Bishop Kurz showed up in all his robes and finery, and we had the full ceremony and Mass with all the traditional paraphernalia, candles, incense and everything. Mr. and Mrs. Tom Newmeier were our witnesses and Bieni was part of the ceremony too. Christian was up in his room crying through the whole service, to be sure he was not left out. We had our third wedding in grand style.

Soon after Christian was born, I got involved with the Hotel Association to represent Dorado Beach in a more political arena. In that group I met Pierre and John Lohner of Swiss Chalet Restaurant and two hotels, the Swiss Chalet and the DaVinci Hotel, in San Juan. We had our European backgrounds in common, and as it turned out, they were interested in hiring me as General Manager of their new hotel in Santurce. This never could have happened in Germany. I wasn't old enough or experienced enough to reach the level of General Manager, and this in my fourth-language country. I couldn't say no.

Chacha and I, Ely and the kids moved out to a beautiful home (which later became a school) close enough for me to walk to work. But after only eighteen months, the Lohner brothers were planning to open a property on St. Croix, back in the U.S. Virgin Islands, and they wanted me to manage it. It was another great opportunity. The Lohner brothers gave me a farewell party, and invited Joel Jennings and Ron Chandler from Rockresorts. I thought it was awfully nice of them to show up and wish me well. After a couple of drinks, Joel and Ron cornered me where nobody else could hear. Joel said, "I don't think you're going to St. Croix."

"What?" I said. "Why not?"

"Cerromar Beach is going to open soon, and Ron is going to be the GM there. We need you to manage Dorado Beach." I nearly fainted. Manager of Dorado Beach Hotel. Now the party was for a whole different reason. The next morning I told the Lohner brothers I was sorry to disappoint them, but I had been offered the chance of a lifetime. Gentlemen that they were, they understood, and we parted on good terms.

Life changed again with my new job title. If I thought I had a busy schedule before, I was mistaken. Now I would learn how much of my life the hotel business could consumed. I was sweating every detail of my job. I wanted every guest to arrive happy and depart happier. If something wasn't perfect, I was furious. If we had a VIP in the house, everybody better know about it, and every single staff person better call him or her by name and, by God, we'd better have their brand of scotch in all the bars. If clouds threatened an important outdoor function or a big golf tournament, I was panicked. It was like swimming against the tide, or worse, like fighting the whirlpool in the river with the pressure holding me down and nowhere to go but up.

It wasn't long before I was smoking three packs of cigarettes a day and drinking rum and Coke at night to sleep. I felt worse and worse, and I started getting a terrible pain in my neck all the time. I figured I had hurt it playing tennis, or spent too much time on the phone, but Chacha sent me to the doctor. Dr. Andreas Salazar said everybody gets a pain in the neck sooner or later, but that we'd take a series of X-rays just in case.

He also told me I had an ulcer and gave me some advice. He said, "Kohler, you've got to stop putting yourself in charge of the weather."

"What?"

"You've got to learn to take it easy. Life is short. You are damaging your health with all the stress in your life. Do something about the things you can do something about, and stop worrying about the things you can't do anything about."

I told myself, Kohler, you have a wonderful wife and two perfect kids. You're just at the beginning of a career with the best hotel company in the greatest business in the world. You have a long way to go and it's time to take care of yourself. On that day, I eliminated the word "stress" from my vocabulary. I quit drinking hard liquor; I stopped smoking cigarettes, and I gave up being in charge of the weather.

A few days later, Dr. Salazar called me back with the X-ray results. He said, "Adi, you are one lucky son of a bitch just to be walking."

"What are you talking about?"

"You've got a broken neck," he said. "The third vertebrae in your neck was fractured years ago. It's become calcified, and that's what's bothering you now."

I told him my story about diving into the Autobahn See.

"Well I don't know what angel's watching over you," said the doctor, "but she's doing a hell of a job."

I couldn't agree with him more.

CHAPTER 19

Mr. Mauna Kea

Early in 1973, I received a telephone call I will never forget. It was Fred Eydt, from the home office in New York. "Adi, would you consider a transfer out of Dorado Beach?" he asked.

I didn't know what to say. Was this good news or bad news? "Fred," I said, "I would like to consider whatever you have on your mind."

"Mauna Kea Beach Hotel."

The words rung in me like a bell. Still, I had no idea the impact they would have on me, and how important they would be to me and my family for the next twenty-seven years of our life.

I didn't consider myself a particularly impulsive person, but when something sounded right, it usually was. Again, I accepted without ever setting foot on the island. I'd met the General Manager, Bob Butterfield, at a corporate meeting a couple of years earlier, and I was confident he and I would work well together, but I didn't know much at all about Hawai'i. I knew it had been a state for about fifteen years, so our blonde-haired, blue-eyed Puerto Rican kids could go to American schools and grow up speaking English. I knew Chacha would love it, and I knew I would be working for Rockresorts, which could always only be first-class. There was nothing difficult about the decision.

The five of us: Chacha and I, Bieni, Christian and Ely, made the long trip from San Juan to Honolulu, first class. On the flight, we toasted our good fortune with champagne, and I suspended the no-

hard-liquor rule to have my first Mai Tai. We finally landed in Honolulu and spent the night at the Beachcomber on Kalakaua Avenue,
where our Wyoming friend Jim Reed was General Manager. The rest
of the family was exhausted, and never left the room, but I was too
excited. I decided to tour around the hotel and make sure Jim was
doing a good job, and of course he was.

Eventually, I ended up at the bar. There was a lady playing the
piano and singing Hawaiian songs. I sat there, sipping the second Mai
Tai of my life, and listened for an hour, thinking it was some of the
most beautiful music I'd ever heard. When she took a break, we introduced ourselves to each other and I learned I'd been enjoying Ms.
Loyal Garner, one of Hawai'i's premier entertainers. I was in love
with Hawaiian music from my first night in Waikiki.

The next morning we left Honolulu on a Hawaiian Airlines flight

Adi relaxes on the plane to Hawaii

for the Big Island's Kamuela Airport. As we approached the island, I looked down to see tiny
white beaches and nothing but
black lava rocks all along the
coast. It looked like the surface
of the moon, not a tropical island. Then we headed inland
and everything turned into my
old favorite color, green. The
little airport was surrounded by
rich farmland and cow pastures (cow was about the last thing I expected to see in Hawai'i.) And it was cold. A misty wind blew across
the tarmack, and for a moment I had a feeling we were in the wrong
place. The sign said "Aloha Waimea." I was told we were to go to
Kamuela.

Then I saw Bob Butterfield walking towards us from the hotel car.
I had no idea he'd come to pick us up himself. "Aloha, Adi," he said
and shook my hand warmly. "Welcome to the Big Island." I made
introductions all around and we left Waimea's bright green fields
heading downhill. "We'll get the family settled in," said Mr. Butterfield,
"then you and I will go on a property tour. We might as well get

started, don't you think?" We drove out of the mist onto a narrow, winding road that twisted past miles of dry, empty land without a building in sight and hardly a tree. I was having trouble imagining a hotel in such a desolate place as the road gradually curved and dropped down closer to the ocean.

At the hotel entrance there was no sign, only a plain stone wall with a bright orange flower and two words: "Mauna Kea." The security guard in his little booth smiled and waved us through. "Good morning, Mr. Butterfield. You must be the Kohler family. Aloha and welcome to Mauna Kea, folks."

We drove past the *lauhala* trees and headed down the narrow road lined with brilliant bougainvillea, towards the sparkling ocean. The golf course sprinklers were on, making fields of rainbows in the grass. We turned past the third hole and pulled up to the front circle, under tall whispering palm trees holding little choirs of singing birds. Everywhere I looked were different flowers. The Bell Captain jumped to open the door. A pretty girl in a flowered dress draped a sweet-smelling *lei* around my neck and gave me a kiss on the cheek. "Welcome to Mr. Mauna Kea," she said, then gasped and giggled. "I'm sorry." She started again, "Welcome to Mauna Kea, Mr. Kohler."

There are moments in your life when you know, beyond the shadow of a doubt, that you are in the right place at the right time. On July 10, 1973, when I stepped across the bridge into the lobby, when I looked across the ocean-blue tiles and saw the three palm trees reaching up to the sky, a whole new world opening up before us, like a living painting of Paradise, I knew. The feeling hit me then and it never left. This was where I was supposed to be.

"Let me show you around."

Bieni, Adi, Chacha and Christian at a Big Island beach

Adi W. Kohler in his best-known position

EPILOGUE

The fat silver moon was slowly approaching the ocean. The restaurant was long since dark. At the table, the near-empty wine bottle lifted to float in chilled water. A tiered tray of candies and *petits fours* tempted the last of the diners with one more bite. The lights in the lounge flicked on bright for the night crew to start cleaning up.

"Mauna Kea and I went through a lot of changes together," Kohler said. "I like to think we have something in common." He carefully considered the colorful chocolate-dipped mac nuts on the top tier, as if he'd been saving one for the end of the story. "She adapted herself to the environment of Hawai'i, and she made herself 'invisible' as Mr. Rockefeller wanted her to be. She embraced and included the people who lived here, without forcing herself on anyone. And she gave them a first-class hotel, a place where they were proud to go to work."

With two fingers he selected a green one, popped it into his mouth and savored the taste for a moment. "She's an older lady now. And maybe she needs a little more cosmetics than she used to, but as you can see I'm completely in love with her. I like to think she cares about me too, in some way. And I think if you can say that about a place then you've done something in your life."

He wiped his two fingers on his napkin, folded it over on the table. "I came from nowhere, from a country that doesn't exist anymore. Where I end up may be nowhere too; I have no way of knowing. But I sure hope it looks like Mauna Kea."

"Last call, gentlemen," said the Restaurant Manager. She held the brandy bottle and the check presenter.

"No, it's late," said Kohler. "Chacha will be wondering what happened to me." He signed with his green pen, stood and stretched.

"Good," she said. "Otherwise I have to leave you here with the ghost."

"What ghost?" said the new Assistant.

"You don't have to worry about the ghost," said Kohler. "He doesn't eat too much."

"Thank you, Adi," he said. "It's been a most enlightening day, and most of the night, I'm afraid. I'm proud to be here, and I hope my family and I will be here for a long time."

"We'll see about that."

"I beg your pardon?"

"My assistants don't tend to stick around all that long. The last four or five are all general managers at first-class hotels, in Hawai'i, on the mainland. One's in Singapore. And they are all extremely successful." He reached into his pocket for the car keys. "You guys are young. Most of your career is in front of you."

He started to walk towards the Lobby; his new Assistant followed. At night, the Mauna Kea took on a whole different, more intimate, aspect, like a candlelit table. Between the pool's blue glow and silver moonlight, palm fronds glittered and whispered among themselves. A sprinkler came on and said, "Shhhhh."

"I'd like to hear more about the Mauna Kea part of your story," he said. "Did you meet a lot of famous people?"

"A few. We had some presidents and vice presidents. The emperor and empress of Japan. A number of movie stars and other people who prefer to remain anonymous." He continued to stride down the corridor. The wide eyes of the Thai dragon seemed to watch them pass.

"What was the worst thing that ever happened to you here? What was the best? How about your most embarrassing moment?"

"There weren't any worst things. Or best," he said. "There were just things." He stopped for a moment, gestured with a wave of his hand. "This is a hotel, brother; not the real world. People come here for a short time and share a little bit of their lives with us, then they go home and tell their own stories the way they want to tell them." He started walking again. "That's what you're going to do, too."

"When you first started here as Manager," he said. "How was it for you? Were you afraid?"

"Afraid of what?" They reached the Lobby. The night auditor waved from his books. Below, Aleka snoozed under his cage cover. The gold *mokala* statues bid them goodnight.

"Afraid that you wouldn't live up to all the expectations, that kind of thing," he said. "That you wouldn't be able to get the job done. That you might not be up to the work."

"No," said Kohler. He lit up a long cigar for the drive home. "Remember, it's not work. It's fun," he said, puffing. "Don't make me have to tell you that again." He smiled and turned toward the dark path to the parking lot.

The new Assistant spotted a matchbook on the curbside, picked it up and put it in his pocket. "Okay, but where do I start?"

"How about the beginning?"

He listened to Kohler's departing footsteps. A fading waft of smoke drifted behind. He heard the car door open and close; the electric window slide down. And Kohler, perhaps to his new Assistant or perhaps to his hotel, said, "Aloha."

Charlot Butterfield, Gov. Nelson and Happy Rockefeller, Bob Butterfield and Adi Kohler

Christian and Adi, getting ready to do their "property walk"

Adi Kohler, high noon

General Manager, mounted

Chacha, Bieni, with blue ribbon, and Adi at Waimea horse show

Christian on Brother

Brother and Adi

Adi with Arnie

Adi with Chi Chi Rodriguez

Golfing with Jim Dent

Escorting Robert Trent Jones, Sr. on an inspection of his golf course

Adi and Laurance S. Rockefeller with a pair of 18th-Century Japanese wooden horses, at their reinstallation into the art collection

Mutti and Adi

Adi receiving the 1987 Resort Executive of the Year award

Bieni stands up for her dad

Kahu and Adi at the Hotel's closing ceremony, in July 1994

Chacha and Adi enjoy a moment to remember

AFTERWORD

The Mauna Kea Beach Hotel

In 1948, while Adi Köhler was waiting tables at his father's restaurant in Oppertshofen, a Mr. Paul Fagan was experimenting with rustic tourism on the island of Maui in what was then the Territory of Hawai'i. In the Caribbean, Laurance S. Rockefeller was taking a swim. And on the other side of the world, a man named Tsutsumi was building his family's future in post-war Tokyo.

Fagan's experiment was a failed sugar plantation in the nearly-inaccessible town of Hana, which he bought with the idea to build a small hotel. From the airport, Hana was a three-hour drive that twisted and curved, climbed, fell and crawled across one-lane bridges, past waterfalls and green jungle that seemed to watch people go by.

He hired a gentleman named Robert Butterfield to manage it. They named it Kau'iki Inn, and when it was ready to open they brought in the baseball team Fagan also owned, the San Francisco Seals (ancestors of the Giants) to christen the hotel. Although the experiment worked for a while, there was something missing. Kau'iki Inn wasn't much more than a boarding house; they decided to offer more. About a year later, they tore it down and re-built it as the visionary Hotel Hana Maui.

There were many things that made it a special place. Its remote location gave guests the feeling of adventure long before they arrived. Its quaint, individual guesthouses were warm and welcoming, immediately offering a sense of ownership and personal care. The rooms were thoughtful, tasteful and designed with the concept of *shibumi,* graceful, simple elegance. There were no phones or televisions to disturb a pervading peacefulness, no air-conditioning to get between a guestroom and the tradewinds, no signs, no commercialism, no hokey *hula* shows or fake *tiki.* Hotel Hana Maui was the quiet Hawai'i.

The Big Island had the same quiet quality. From the time it was "discovered" by Captain James Cook late in the 18th Century until the Japanese attack on Pearl Harbor, life was slow-paced and relatively peaceful (despite ongoing feuds between warring chiefs). The island might have been overlooked by tourists except for the novelty of a Volcanic eruption at Kilauea.

Benjamin Pitman, husband of High Chiefess Kinoole, built a thatched hut over a steam vent and charged a dollar a night for visitors to the crater. It grew into a legendary hotel, Volcano House, which hosted famous American travelers like Mark Twain, who fell in love with the Island and wrote extensively about his experiences. But the long trip by steamship and horseback was not for the casual sightseer.

Important moments in Hawaiian history took place on the Big Island. It is where King Kamehameha I was born, where he built his great temple and united the islands under one kingdom, and where he died. It is where Captain Cook dropped anchor and introduced the *haole* (Caucasian) to the island. It is also the place where he was killed.

On the Big Island, missionaries commissioned the first Christian Church in Hawaii, and the ancient *kapu* system was banned forever. *Haole* business interests began to purchase large tracts of the *aina* (land), an alien concept for Hawaiians. Huge agricultural ventures grew along the rainy coastal regions. In Honolulu, the last reigning queen of the monarchy, Liliuokalani, was deposed by American capitalists and life changed forever for Kamehameha's united Hawai'i. Despite such drastic movement around them, most people lived quietly in the traditional way, as fishermen or farmers, while their culture shifted from a subsistence system to an economic one.

Early in the 20th Century, more than 250,000 acres in the center of the island belonged to Parker Ranch, the world's largest privately-owned cattle ranch, originally a royal grant to American sailor John Palmer Parker, who landed at Kawaihae about 1861 and later married Kamehameha's granddaughter, Kipikana. In many ways, Parker Ranch was the second "hotel" on the Big Island, since it had the grandest house and most elegant facilities, located just outside the little paniolo (cowboy) town of Waimea. The Parker family welcomed foreign royalty, American celebrities and politicians, and otherwise played host as a center of Island society.

Outside the ranch, most people worked for one of the huge sugar cane plantations which dominated the former chiefdoms. Plantation workers came to the Island in immigration waves, from China, Japan, Korea, the Philippines, Portugal and Puerto Rico. They lived on the plantation proper in "camps," designated by ethnicity at first and family later. Women and men worked mostly manual labor jobs in exchange for a wage, housing, medical care, schooling for their children, social and church activities, and a ration of hope that their lives on the Big Island would be better than where they'd come from. In the 1940's, second and third-generation citizens of the plantations were dependents of the sugar cane culture.

During World War II, more than 50,000 US troops hit the Big Island for training after the battle of Tarawa, a disastrous loss in the Pacific Theater. In March 1942, Parker Ranch manager Hartwell Carter loaned thousands of acres to Uncle Sam at no charge. The military built "Camp Tarawa" in the fields outside of Waimea town, and started training for a battle called Iwo Jima. The sudden population boom sparked a rush of private enterprise. Hamburger stands, laundry services and other businesses for soldiers opened up their doors and welcomed the *malihini* (strangers) to town. Local *paniolo* (cowboys) challenged soldiers from Montana and Wyoming in the town's first official rodeo, and Parker School became the USO Club. It was a very busy time, which helped distract worried people from thoughts of family members fighting elsewhere, or Japanese relatives in internment camps on the mainland.

When the war was over, the Big Island had changed. Although it was still sleepy and slow-moving, it was infected with a new spirit of capitalism and a sense of belonging to the United States. Plus, America had discovered Hawai'i after Pearl Harbor, and a new tourist industry bloomed in Waikiki. Eventually, some of that prosperity spread out to the neighbor islands, but the Big Island was slow to catch up. By the time Hawai'i turned from a Territory into a State in 1959, only a few hotels in Hilo and Kona opened doors for new visitors, leaving the rest of the island to do what they always had done.

At the same time it was becoming obvious that the sugar cane economy would not last forever, as less-expensive sugar started being produced in Mexico, the Philippines and elsewhere. Although it was a few years in the future, the government of Hawai'i saw a serious problem on the way. Not only was its main source of income drying up, its large population of unskilled laborers, many of whom barely spoke English, were soon going to be without not just a job, but a lifestyle. It was a time ripe for change.

Laurance Spelman Rockefeller's family name was synonymous with wealth and philanthropy. "LSR," son of John D. Rockefeller, Jr. and brother of Governor Nelson Rockefeller, had a personal mission that took a slightly different course from the rest of the family; his focus was on conservation. By purchasing thousands of acres of wilderness in the United States and then establishing them as national parks, LSR successfully guaranteed the protection of certain wildlife and forests, and the experience of natural America for many future generations.

LSR believed that money carefully inserted into the right area at the right time would blossom and grow into self-sustaining, even profitable, enterprise. Some say he invented the concept of "venture capitalism."

Mr. Rockefeller was first interested in hotels as lodging in his wilderness areas in Wyoming. When his theory worked and the properties grew to be successful, he moved into other areas. In 1948, he sailed northward through the Caribbean on his private yacht, according to him "looking for a good place to swim," along almost every island between Venezuela and Puerto Rico. When he dropped an-

chor off St. John in the U.S. Virgin Islands, he discovered Caneel Bay
Plantation, in a similar way to Paul Fagan's discovery of Hana, Maui.
In 1952, he purchased the old sugar cane operation with a small hotel, along with 5,000 surrounding acres. He donated these back to
the country as the U.S. Virgin Islands National Park. He also began
plans to build Caneel Bay Plantation, which opened two years later.

"Every great beach deserves a great hotel," he said once. When
Caneel was on its feet, he moved on to other great beach sites including Little Dix Bay on Virgin Gorda in the British Virgin Islands. Then
he explored Puerto Rico, found an old grapefruit plantation and began planning Dorado Beach Hotel. This project was part of the
country's "Operation Bootstrap," a program of expanding tourism
outwards from San Juan. Dorado opened in 1958, with plans already
in place for its sister, Cerromar.

In 1960, Mr. and Mrs. Rockefeller, along with Mr. and Mrs. Walter
Collins of the construction company Belt, Collins & Associates, Ltd.,
visited Hotel Hana Maui. Bob Butterfield showed him around the place,
answering his many questions and enjoying the intelligence and en-
thusiasm of this remarkable man.

"Where do you get the flowers?" he asked. Butterfield said they
used to truck them in, but they'd worked with local farmers to start
growing what they needed. "How do you get by without air-conditioning? Where does the water come from? What do guests do when
it rains? How do you get along with one single dining room? Where
does the staff live?" He wanted to know everything. For the next
several years, LSR would call Butterfield now and then, asking more
questions, keeping in touch, checking on Hotel Hana Maui's success,
and whether or not they ever got air-conditioning.

In June of that same year, the governor of Hawai'i, William F. Quinn,
invited LSR to visit the Big Island. The coastal area of the South Kohala
District had the earmarks of Mr. Rockefeller's signature projects: a
picturesque setting that merited conservation and, with the increas-
ing decline of the sugar cane industry, an economic *puka* (hole) that
needed filling. It had all the elements of a match made in heaven.

It bears mentioning that also in 1948, far to the west, a Mr. Yasujiro Tsutsumi, founding patriarch of one of the world's wealthiest families, was doing everything in his power to grow his own business. Driving himself and his company very hard, he had built a railroad out of almost nothing. In response to Tokyo's rapidly-growing need for a way to haul sewage out of the city, he made the family fortune shovelling, for want of a better word, fertilizer.

Governor Quinn invited LSR to visit the Big Island in June 1960. They toured a number of potential development sites, including several owned by Parker Ranch. The Ranch was going through changes too, and had recently decided to expand their business by leasing out some of their land holdings. A particular parcel in the South Kohala District along the beach at Kauna'oa Bay, known locally as "Parker Ranch Beach," was prime oceanfront real estate, although it had nothing to support it, zero infrastructure: no road, no water, sewer, telephone or power lines. They hiked down a rocky trail in the hot sun, past scrubby *kiawe* (mesquite) bushes and tangle of *naupaka* (a Hawaiian shrub) laced with *kauna'oa* (orange dodder). At the end of the trail was a perfect crescent of white sand and an inviting stretch of turquoise ocean. Mr. Rockefeller asked if he could go in for a swim.

What was he thinking that sunny afternoon in the water? He'd done it at Dorado, but at least there the main tourist center, San Juan, was on the same island. Honolulu was an hour away by air, and the nearest airport was in Hilo, a ninety-minute drive. He'd done it at Caneel, but at least the island of St. John had some rain. Here, they were lucky to get nine inches in a year. Other than the beach, Kauna'oa Bay was lava rock, brush and more lava rock. There was nothing here to work with, but one great beach.

Old Hawaiians may have used the beach for canoe storage, and *ali'i* (chiefs) may have surfed there in the winter months, or camped overnight on their way to somewhere else. But even they would take advantage of beaches with better accessibility at Kawaihae or Anaeho'omalu, and leave Kauna'oa undisturbed. Some legends say that Kauna'oa Bay was a kind of mystic place, where the *aumakua* (ancestral deities) crossed between the spirit world and ours. Maybe one of them whispered in Mr. Rockefeller's ear that day. In any case, when he was in the water and looked up at the summit of Mauna Kea (white mountain), he must have had that sense of being in the right place at the right time.

LSR signed a ninety-nine-year lease with Parker Ranch for 1,800 acres and established the Olohana Corporation to evaluate development potential for the Queen Emma Estate and Ouli lease lands adjacent to the property. He also purchased the "White House," a former ranch manager's home twelve miles uphill in Waimea, to accommodate visitors while the hotel was completed.

The company was named after English advisor to Kamehameha I, John Young, who lived in Kawaihae. "Olohana" was his nickname, from the Hawaiian-ized way of mimicking his call to work: "All hands!" Olohana Corporation's initial long-range plan was to build two hotels, two golf courses, a large residential community, shopping arcade and cultural center. According to Les Moore, LSR envisioned Kawaihae "as the third largest city in Hawaii with shipping, fishing, services and housing developments booming." The master plan also included landing pad for hovercraft, which they saw as the most logical interisland transportation in the future.

While the Mauna Kea Beach Hotel was still in the design phase, LSR brought in a brilliant young historian, Russell Apple to survey and map the entire area for archeological sites. Mr. Rockefeller was ultimately concerned with conservation, and this included human culture as well as natural resources. They were relieved to learn that other than a small fishing shrine along the coast, a *honu*, turtle deity carving at Kaaha Point and a few stone shelters that might have been used as house walls or cattle pens, the property held no significant sites. Apple believed the beautiful beach was just that, a recreation area, possibly a place for canoe storage or camping along the "King's Trail" from Kona to Kohala. It was safe, historically, to build there.

Another important archeological site was nearby, however. Pu'ukohola Heiau, adjacent to the property, was a major symbol in Hawaiian history. In 1791 the chief priest of King Kamehameha the Great advised him he would rule all the islands of Hawai'i if he built (or some say re-built) a *heiau* (temple) on this spot. Said to be the last site in Hawai'i for the performance of human sacrifice, the massive lava stone temple was built by thousands of warriors, passing rocks hand-to-hand. Its completion marked Kamehameha's conquest and unified rule of the islands as one kingdom. In keeping with his conservationist philosophy, Mr. Rockefeller had Pu'ukohola restored and donated to the National Park Service as a National Historic Site. (On Maui, he also worked with pilot Charles Lindbergh to expand Haleakala National Park.)

For his own monumental work, the San Francisco branch of Skidmore, Owings and Merrill (SOM) was hired to design the Mauna Kea Beach Hotel. This noted architectural firm was founded in 1936 in New York by Louis Skidmore, Nathaniel Owings and John O. Merrill. They were the best, in accordance with the Rockefeller tradition of "experting," getting the best people to give the best thought and effort to any project.

LSR's main requirement was that the hotel intrude on the natural surroundings as little as possible. The design should follow the natural contours of the land, incorporate materials of the region (in this case, lava rock) and in every possible way make the hotel "invisible."

One of the first things LSR did was install a weather station on the site in order to test his pet theory: was it possible to operate a resort in a tropical climate, without air-conditioning? The weather station proved that a cool, onshore breeze could be depended upon during the days and an offshore breeze blew down from the mountains at night.

Nat Owings approached Mr. Rockefeller with an idea for individual cottages along the beach; the boss loved it. Allston Boyer, LSR's associate who oversaw the management of his resorts, said it was "A pretty weird-looking thing. It resembled a miniature mosque... It featured a big hole in the ceiling, right over the bathtub, so you could lie there, I guess, and stare at the sky, praying, maybe, that a face wouldn't suddenly appear at the edge. It also had a large opening in the main ceiling that was partially covered by something that looked like a cereal bowl turned upside down. This was designed to keep rain out, but let air in and out." LSR loved the idea of individual cottages and was extremely excited about the natural cooling system.

They built a model cottage near the beach. Allston Boyer and Bob Hoke from the New York office spent two long, windless nights sweltering in the model, but LSR was convinced that it would work, and pushed ahead with the plan to build 100 units. Mother Nature had other ideas. Twice, tropical storms blew up the coast while architects and contractors were visiting. The little house was all but washed away. The plan was dumped; the dome on the beach gently dissembled by a D-9 bulldozer. The architects literally went back to the drawing board to design a single building, one which could combine the advantages of independent units with the convenience, and cost-savings, of a master one.

The golf course came first. Robert Trent Jones (Senior) had built Dorado's golf course, so in 1962 LSR brought him to the Mauna Kea site. They stood on a craggy bluff overlooking what is now the Third Hole. LSR said, "Trent, can you build a golf course here?"

He replied, "Mr. Rockefeller, if you allow me to build a golf course here, this'll be the most beautiful hole in the world."

Jones was born in Liverpool after his parents left Rhyl, Wales. They came to America when he was four years old. He learned to play and appreciate golf in Rochester, New York and created the entire field of golf architecture by combining the studies of agriculture, agronomy, engineering, surveying, business management, accounting and sketching. (Jones designed or re-designed over 500 golf courses before his death in Fort Lauderdale Florida in the year 2000, including his first, the Peachtree in Atlanta in 1948, and the White House putting green for President Eisenhower. In 1987 he was inducted into the Golf World Hall of Fame.) Robert Trent Jones, like SOM, was the best.

Following LSR's instructions about Mauna Kea's overall design vision, Jones decided to bulldoze as little as possible, using natural elevations for the tees and existing pockets for the greens. But the first problem was lava. Jones had made grass grow in the sand at Dorado, but this was something else again. He took a sample of rock, crushed it with a hammer and was convinced the fine dust would make a good soil base. The *a'a* (rough, crumbly lava) had the same porous properties as the coral. It was going to work and he decided to prove it.

In 1964, he hired a Hawai'i man, Robert Itamoto, to be the golf course superintendent. A graduate of Colorado State University, Itamoto was the only person in Hawai'i who had experience (at the Naval Air Station at Barber's Point) with the "greens quality" hybrid Bermuda grasses Jones wanted to use (Arizona Bermuda on the fairways and roughs, Tifton 328 on the greens).

Itamoto was intrigued by the offer and the challenge and decided to take a look at the site. When he arrived on the island, Jones sent a Jeep to bring him the twelve miles downhill. Itamoto looked around and said, "Why in the world would Mr. Rockefeller want to build a hotel in a place like this?" Jones laughed and started to explain. Itamoto decided to take the job and get the grass growing, then go back to Honolulu and work at a real golf course. He stayed at Mauna Kea almost forty years.

He and Jones leveled a ten-acre test area and drilled an irrigation well. They laid down four inches of crushed lava and topped it off with three inches of crushed coral, then seeded and began to water over a million gallons a day in the beginning. Two months later it was green.

Robert Trent Jones hit the first ball when the course was finished from the spectacular Third Tee. Bob Itamoto played the course all by himself one afternoon, just before it opened. He remembers it was not what he expected. "Before Mauna Kea," he said, "golf courses were essentially flat. Not that challenging and interesting. The greens weren't so big and there were not as many bunkers. Plus 7,000 yards is a huge golf course." There wasn't anything like it anywhere.

Their achievement immediately earned attention from other golf developers. Itamoto says that almost every golf course in Hawai'i started planting that hybrid Bermuda grass. When Mr. Rockefeller saw the course he was pleased. He had only one requirement: Itamoto had to promise to keep it 98% free of weeds. He did.

The course was officially christened in December 1964 with a "Big Three" match play between Jack Nicklaus, Gary Player and Arnold Palmer. The event was filmed by Music Corporation of America as part of an eight-match series for NBC, which introduced the Mauna Kea to its audience a year before the Hotel opened.

Jack Nicklaus won, and the story is that Gary Player found the Third Hole a little too challenging. However, according to the *Honolulu Star-Bulletin*, all three golf giants deferred to the next-forward tee. In fact, the first man to hit the green from the 250-yard tee was Juan Chi Chi Rodriguez, twice in a row, to within ten feet of the pin. After the opening match, Trent Jones consulted with Rockefeller and they moved the tee forward to make it accessible to golfers of all levels. (It's since been restored to its original position.)

While Mauna Kea's grass was getting greener, the new, single building began to take shape, first on paper. Skidmore Owings Merrill always took on projects as a firm, and credit for their work went to the entire team. Although architect Edward Charles Bassett played a bigger role, he did not appreciate personal recognition. In one interview, he said it was a myth to think "that a building could be born full-blown out of a single person's head."

SOM and Bassett took Mr. Rockefeller's new direction very seriously and studied the site not only physically, but with regards to culture, tradition and spirituality. They brought elements of East and West together from the very beginning, drawing on both the modernistic work of Frank Lloyd Wright and the simple *shibumi* style of the Japanese. They used clean, geometric lines and flat planes to create three "floating" stories supported by massive, rough-finish concrete pillars around a huge atrium, making space more important than structure.

Haas and Haynie were the general contractors; they had eighty-seven subcontractors. Belt, Collins & Associates, Ltd. was the engineering-planning company, and Walter Collins played an important role in many of the initial decisions. (A plaque mounted near the Hau Tree restaurant testifies to his contribution.) Eckbo, Dean, Austin & Williams of San Francisco was the landscape architect. Makiki Nursery, under the direction of owner Wilbert Choi, planted 149,000 trees and shrubs on the property, including four palm trees hoisted over the three-story walls by crane. They were planted on the Promenade under Hawaii's very first motorized skylight.

A battalion of work crews and equipment moved in, established a perimeter and dug in. Dining facilities were built to feed 500 workers three hot meals every day, and extra refrigeration was added to store fish caught by the men *pau hana* (after work). 54,000 square feet of Mexican shale, 5,000 square feet of Italian marble and 30,000 square feet of local lava went into the Hotel, along with a mile of Narra wood, eleven miles of pipe, 1,700 tons of reinforcing steel and 20,242 cubic yards of concrete. For the roof, they trucked in black beach pebbles from a location ninety miles away. Altogether more than 1,500,000 man hours went into the hotel infrastructure, buildings and golf course.

Every effort was made to keep guests in touch with nature and make the buildings "invisible." At first, the exteriors were painted a glowing "Pueblo white," but that was changed to match the color of sand on the beach. The original dining room, The Pavilion, had a three-tiered seating area to provide ocean views from almost every chair, with soaring plate glass walls on all four sides of a simple, rectangular room with dark wood floors and twenty-foot ceilings. A wide patio of Mexican shale on the ocean-side allowed the option of eating breakfast or dinner outdoors. The Terrace, where the signature luncheon buffet would be served, was a restaurant with no walls at all, just tables set among the towering pillars with a breathtaking ocean overlook.

It was impossible to stay indoors at Mauna Kea. Guest rooms opened up onto atrium gardens instead of closed corridors. The lobby was practically wall-less and ceiling-less, open to blue sky above, terraced gardens below, the mountains behind and the vast blue Pacific just beyond. The final decision was to provide the rooms with air-conditioning, but also give them large *lanai* (balconies) with sliding glass doors as well as screen doors and wooden louvered doors on both sides to allow cross ventilation. Thus guests had the option of turning Mr. Rockefeller's detested air-conditioning on, or not.

He may have lost the air-conditioning battle, but he won the TV war. The rooms did not have televisions or radios. He wanted peace and quiet and he wanted people to go outside and play. "What we look for," he said once, "are people who have enough inner resources to enjoy an unorganized environment, to appreciate peace, serenity, beauty and reasonable comfort...We expect to draw outdoor-minded people, people who want to get away from organized activities."

To accomplish LSR's intentions on the inside as well as the outside, Skidmore Owings Merrill hired New York-based interior decorator Davis Allen, who had done Dorado Beach. If SOM had a difficult job in designing an "invisible" building, Allen's was equally tough. LSR wanted to bring elements of East and West together in a fusion of styles. That itself was an interesting challenge. He also intended to use a bright, tropical palette (turquoise, lime green, yellow and tangerine) inside the guestrooms. He commissioned Honolulu artist Lloyd Sexton to paint a series of watercolors in those hues, and a matching print would hang in each room.

If that wasn't enough, LSR also planned to place over 1,600 pieces of Asian and Pacific artwork throughout the public areas. He had already contracted Meali'i Kalama and the ladies of Honolulu's Kawaiahao Church, under the direction of Reverend Abraham Akaka, to hand-sew Hawaiian quilts to hang in the open corridors. Sixty million stitches went into thirty original designs, each with its own name and story to tell. After months of intricate work, the ladies met their deadline, and re-donated LSR's generous commission to Kawaiahao Church. A one-of-a-kind Hawaiian flag quilt in red, white and blue was their gift to Mr. Rockefeller. (Mrs. Kalama was honored as one of America's "living treasures" with a National Folk Arts Heritage Award in 1985.)

(The art pieces, especially the quilts, deserve their own story which has already been written by Professor Don Aanavi in his beautiful book The Art of Mauna Kea, designed by Barbara Pope and published by the East West Center and Mauna Kea Beach Hotel in 1989, in process of being reprinted by Mauna Kea Resort.)

Davis Allen filled the Mauna Kea with treasures: handcrafted willow headboards from Milan, teak night-tables, Hawaiian lauhala mats, handmade Thai bedspreads, Irish cotton beach towels with Hawaiian petroglyph designs, Lloyd Sexton lithographs printed in Paris, and Japanese pottery. Each room featured a built-in ice cube maker (later

replaced with the familiar black plastic insulated ice buckets). Every
piece was run by Skidmore Owings and Merrill first, who were in the
unique situation of having LSR's trust, and therefore total control over
the entire Mauna Kea concept. Each element of design was approved
by them, which is why the finished project had such a smooth, coordinated look. Everything had to work together.

The process was painstaking, as the design team moved step by
step, analyzing every move a guest would make, and anticipating every need. Arrive, unpack, bathe, change, sleep, wake, eat, drink.
"Okay, you can put suitcases here, but we need to add a hook for a
garment bag. You hang shirts and jackets here, long gowns here.
You need this much closet space and this many dresser drawers for a
two-week stay. You need a rack to hang wet swimsuits on the bal-
cony. We need a lamp at the writing table and lights for reading in
bed, but they all need three-way switches so you can turn them on
and off from the source or at the doorway. You need candles and a
book of matches in the nightstand drawer, just in case."

The bathrooms were a project in themselves. "You shave, you
need a towel ring by the sink. You take a shower, you need a high-
pressure shower head, towel bars by the bathtub, grab bars and a
soap dish that drains properly." It's interesting to imagine fully-clothed
executives, standing in the bathtub and going through the motions
again and again. When the final layout was complete, it was Mr.
Rockefeller who noticed there was no place to put a toothbrush.
Davis Allen custom-ordered rough-fired blue clay mugs from Japan
and two were placed in each bath.

Needham and Groman, the company who designed LSR's previous resort logos, developed the simplistic and ultimately recogniz-
able orange plumeria, which decorated so many hotel items. Mr.
Rockefeller's resorts all had very basic, iconic logo designs in one
flat, solid color. When the team of New York designers came in to
get a feel for the property, they were overwhelmed by the bright,
energetic colors in the sunsets and flowering trees, which Davis Allen
had reflected in the guest rooms. To communicate this essence to an
American market, they chose the simple elegance of the plumeria
flower in bright orange.

If the logo was never actually engraved in stone, it was certainly painted, carved, embossed, etched and printed onto almost everything else. It bloomed everywhere, from delicate porcelain teapots to the tail of a bright yellow Cessna which delivered VIPs to Kamuela Airport. It decorated aloha shirts, swimming shorts, shower caps, ties, trays, tees and golf caps, and miniature flashlights for getting around in the subdued night lighting. And it was never allowed to vary. The particular orange was PMS #165 and nothing else. The plumeria had exactly five petals, which curved gently clockwise, with the bottom two petals sitting on the "horizon." It's said that LSR designed the orange and white logo matchboxes himself.

The Milici Advertising Agency, one of the top three firms in the state, received the advertising and public relations account. Ms. Bobby Hughes, Milici's vice president and director of public relations, took on the PR job. It was she who made the manta rays into Mauna Kea's evening stars. The rays swam along the rocky shoreline every night to feed on plankton which were attracted to the artificial lights. When she wrote about strolling down to Manta Ray Pointe to watch their magical "dance," she created an after-dinner tradition which exists to this day.

Mr. Leslie Moore, a Cornell graduate who ran Caneel Bay for eight years, was brought in as General Manager along with his wife Betty, characterized by her long, braided hair. When he was in the Navy during WWII, he put ashore on the Kohala Coast and fell in love with the beach then. During construction, the Moore's made sandwiches for the golfers and hosted Mr. Rockefeller's VIP guests at the White House. Richard Erb and James Reed were his two executive assistants.

After extensive interview sessions in Kamuela, Hilo and the University of Hawai'i Extension Service in Kainaliu, the Mauna Kea opened fully-staffed with 325 employees and a $750,000 annual payroll. Priority was given to Big Island residents who were not working, and of the nearly 500 who applied for twenty different kinds of jobs, only fifteen people lived elsewhere. "This is a community hotel," said Leslie Moore, "and we are hiring people who we hope will stay with us permanently."

Clay James headed the Food and Beverage Department, and Chef Walter Blum ran the kitchen, described by *Star Bulletin* writer Cobey Black as "the size of the commuters' level at Grand Central Station." Originally from Switzerland, Chef Blum first came to the U.S. for the Swiss Pavilion at the 1939 New York World's Fair. He worked in Cairo, Egypt, the New York Ritz Carlton, the Greenbrier and the Arizona Biltmore, and spent the previous ten summers with the Grand Teton Lodge Company in Jackson Hole, Wyoming. There was no one better for the job. He worked closely with the architects to create a kitchen that was "well-balanced. About as perfect as a kitchen might be."

Specializing in French, German and Spanish cuisine, he began experimenting with Hawaiian and oriental dishes. He and Les Moore worked closely with the local farmers to develop the fresh produce they needed for the menus. One story says that Moore, at a community meeting with the farmers, stood up and drew a dollar sign on the blackboard. "Does anyone here read music?" he said.

Bob Itamoto was already bringing up his "baby" golf course. Plans were in place to have Hawai'i golf legend Ted Makalena, winner of every major tournament in the state as Head Pro, along with Harold "Rags" Ragland and Hawai'i's "first lady of golf," Jackie Pung (Women's Pro). Dale Hendrickson would supervise the golf course. At the time, Mauna Kea was represented by the PGA's leading money winner Jack Nicklaus on the professional tour. Nicklaus called Mauna Kea "more fun to play than any course I know."

Other sports personalities included *paniolo* guide Leroy Lindsey at the stables in Waimea, game hunter Patrick Cootey, Tennis Pro Henry Kamakana (on the "cork-turf" courts), beach expert Clifford Hannah and deepsea fisherman Frenchie Dupree.

Big Island resident Albert C. "Slim" Holt's company was named the official transportation agent, shuttling guests from Hilo, Kona and Kamuela airports to the Hotel by Cadillac limousines, eleven-passenger "stretchouts" and deluxe motor coaches. He also guided sightseeing tours.

To their credit, the company hired capable local women into key posts. Mrs. Piilani Bell, LSR's housekeeper at the White House, put the Housekeeping department together and the concept of dirt vanished from the Mauna Kea. Molly Mehau (holder of the 1955 "Women's Largest Marlin" trophy) handled reservations, Queenie Dowsett directed the entertainers and Waimea teacher Thelma Lindsey was Personnel Director. Mrs. Martha Jones trained the waitstaff, one step at a time, from fingernails to shoe polish, tray-walking, talking, pouring, serving, table-setting and always, always smiling. A Swedish woman, Elije Junte, was Sommelier, one of the very few females at that level. Many, many other women (and men too) helped make sure Mauna Kea was "experted" to Mr. Rockefeller's standard.

When it was time to open the doors, it looked like a miracle had happened at Kauna'oa Bay. Mr. Rockefeller had not only preserved the natural surroundings, he'd made them better, perhaps as good as they could be. Someone asked him later if the site at Kauna'oa had not been available at the time, would he have built his Hawai'i project somewhere else. He said, "Oh I doubt it. Mauna Kea was the *right* spot."

The Hotel had three openings. The first was scheduled for Friday, July 2, 1965, just for the Big Island community. Hundreds of people drove down the hill to see the new hotel they'd heard so much about. At the last minute, Mother Nature decided to remind everyone who was in charge. There was a *tsunami* warning, and they had to send everyone home. Fortunately, the tidal wave never came and the festivities were rescheduled and successfully held on the Fourth of July.

The second event was July 24, when Mr. and Mrs. Rockefeller welcomed 700 invited guests into the Mauna Kea for a Grand Opening ceremony. The distinguished guest list included political and hospitality notables, community leaders and a contingent of Waimea society to rival Parker Ranch's finest gala.

Hawaii Tribune Herald writer Maxine C. Hughes took note of "the Asa Baldwins, the Kenneth Browns, the Harrison Cooks, the Ben Dillinghams, the Robert Belts, Dr. and Mrs. Leo Bernstein, the Douglas Guilds, the Richard Lymans, the Lyman-Perry-Fiskes, the Lloyd Sextons, the Gilliard Smarts, the Philip Spaldings, Mrs. William Roth, Barbara Thompson, the Herold Veidigs, the Boyd MacNaughtons, the William Maus and innumerable others." (She also reports that "Mrs.

Rockefeller received in a pastel print shift with which she wore short white gloves.") Also in attendance were the country's three top airlines executives: Floyd Hall of Eastern, Terrell Drinkwater of Western and William Patterson of United Air Lines. (It was the first landing in Hilo by a United airliner.)

Guests wore beautiful red and yellow *lei lehua* made by Mrs. John Lekelessa. As they stepped into the sun-illuminated "floating" lobby, a pair of glittering gilded *mokala,* disciples of the Buddha, flanked the entrance, where tiles the color of liquid sapphire poured across the room and out to sea. To use the vernacular of the day, it blew them away. Nobody had seen anything like it before.

Reverend Abraham K. Akaka, Pastor of Kawaiahao Church in Honolulu, blessed the Hotel. "Kahu" reminded the audience these were

"Kabu," Rev. Abraham Akaka and Mrs. Mary Lou Akaka

ancient lands, chosen by aumakua to enter and leave the spirit world. "For centuries, this place has been a Hawaiian wilderness," he said. "… the place where the mystery and majesty, the beauty and glory of God are to be found, the place where the gods and demigods chose to begin a new thing in the spirit and life of man. Old problems are solved and new questions are answered in the wilderness. It is the Gateway of the Soul of man to God."

He held a *koa* bowl that once belonged to King Kamehameha the Great, passed down to his hand from the family of Keauhulihia Humeku, chief of Waimea. It was filled with water from the ancient springs of Kawaiahao, which he sprinkled with a *ti* leaf onto the ground, saying, "I anoint and set apart the Mauna Kea Beach Hotel to the glory of God, and to the Joy, Peace and Well-being of man, *ma ka inoa o ka Makua, ke Keiki, ame ka Uhane Hemolele.* Amen."

In the pause that followed, there may have been only the sound of ocean.

Kahu essentially "invented" the tradition of blessing new businesses in Hawai'i, and performed the ceremony for hundreds of important buildings statewide. He had a custom of saying it was Chinese tradition to set off fireworks following a prayer, so the gods would pay attention. "We don't have any firecrackers here," he said. "But if we clap our hands together very loud, they just might hear." The applause would be thunderous.

Mr. Rockefeller's remarks follow.

"May I express the hope and faith that all of us now here and all who come as future guests of the Mauna Kea Beach Hotel will leave in some way renewed in body and spirit.

"May we all find inspiration in the majesty of the sea and the beauty of the surrounding mountains. May we learn again the joy of living and that goodwill is the key to brotherly love.

"May we recognize anew that material goods are but the means, stepping stones, to the spiritual meaning and purpose of life.

"May we restore our faith in the wisdom of the philosopher who wrote 'To seek God is already to find Him.'

"And finally, may we find here greater awareness, faith and belief in the oneness, the eternal unity of God, Man and Nature.

"Thank you again for your presence here on this occasion, it means much more to Mrs. Rockefeller and myself than we can readily find words to express.

"Before you at the table is a medallion which I hope will serve as an appropriate reminder of a pleasant occasion, of our gratitude, and of the warmth and sincerity of our good wishes to all of you, and to all of those people who come here in the future.

"Aloha."

The third opening followed the main dedication luncheon, as twenty of the 154 guest rooms received the Rockefellers' invited guests. They hosted a weekend series of extravagant events including the "First Mauna Kea Handicap Tournament," a Volcano sightseeing tour, Hawaiian arts demonstrations, horseback riding, mountain hunting and deep-sea fishing excursions aboard the Vici, Goodbye Charlie or the Dorado out of Kawaihae Harbor.

An elaborate *lu'au* on Friday and formal party on Saturday featured Hawaii's top entertainers. Albert Nahale'a wrote a song "Hale Kipa Mauna Kea" especially for the occasion. The Hilo Kalimas played a specialty number featuring the seldom-seen *pupuhi*/conch shell, *ohe hano*/nose flute and *ka'eke'eke*/bamboo pipe organ. The program read like a roster of stars: Danny Kaleikini, Haunana Kahalewai, Iolani Luahine, Ida Nauone, Pierson Thal, Hilo Hattie, the Pua Melia Trio, Joseph Kahalalio Trio and Ken Alford's Dixiecrats Orchestra.

Local and national travel writers were inspired. Howard Pierce wrote in the *Hawaii Tribune Herald*, "This favored companion of the crescent beach is all at once a *hale ho'okipa* (guest house), *hale ali'i* (chief's house), *hale aina* (eating house), *hale halawai* (meeting house), *halehale* (high, towering), *hale manu* (aviary) and *hale noa* (house without tabu where all mingle.)

"Mauna Kea Beach Hotel qualifies, too, with little stretch of the imagination as *hale lana* (floating house) for by virtue of its open construction it seems to float over and amid its garden site, truly an Aladdin's magic carpet. It can be termed in all truth, with no stretch of the imagination, *hale lani* (heavenly house) and *hale nani* (house of beauty).

"But however any one individual may judge this new equation in travel hospitality and aloha, Mauna Kea Beach Hotel will be to all people who come within its spell an unforgettable pause in their lives, a symbol of the very best having been made better."

Caskie Stinnett wrote for *Holiday*, "For a long time now I have stubbornly held to the view that anything Laurance S. Rockefeller can do, God can do as well. But my first glance from a plane window at Mauna Kea…caused me a moment's hesitation. If nothing else, one had certainly picked up nicely where the Other had left off." After a lavish description of the grounds, buildings, beach and facilities, Stinnett concludes with, "After this, I presume, Mr. Rockefeller rested."

Jerry Hulse, *Los Angeles Times*, said "Mr. Rockefeller built a dream house, a magnificent monument dedicated to the sun-worshipping cult and golfers everywhere. By comparison, the Beverly Hills Hotel would rank as a home for the indigent."

Leavitt F. Morris, of the *Christian Science Monitor*, wrote, "I have been asked many times… When are you going to the moon? 'Never,' I have replied. But today I must revise that answer on one condition. If Mr. Rockefeller decides to build a hotel on the moon then I would want to go there to see it!"

The Mauna Kea Beach Hotel was the costliest resort hotel ever built. Fifteen million dollars (over $100,000 per room) was unheard of. The golf course was an additional $2,000,000. The completed building received the Honor Award of the American Institute of Architects and was named one of *Fortune* magazine's "Ten Best Buildings of 1966." In 1967, *Esquire* listed The Mauna Kea, The Plaza in New York and The Gritti Palace in Venice, as the three greatest hotels in the world.

To help put this in perspective, Claridge's in London was number six, the Kahala Hilton in Honolulu was number fifteen and The Paris Ritz was number twenty-seven. Mr. Inumaru's Imperial Hotel in Tokyo was number fourteen. (This remarkable building was demolished that same year.)

The room rates in 1965 were a whopping $43-48 per night on the Modified American Plan, breakfast and dinner included. A round of golf was eight dollars. Club membership was fifty dollars. The Hotel's first "Honeymoon Special" included four nights, a bottle of champagne and transportation to and from the airport, for $240. During the first three months of operation, occupancy averaged 72%; after that it climbed into the nineties and stayed there.

On August 1, 1966, about a year after opening, Mr. Robert Butterfield came over from Hotel Hana Maui, after eighteen years, to be Mauna Kea's General Manager, joined by his wife Charlot and their two children. "Mr. B" was also a Cornell graduate, with a long string of hospitality credentials. Leslie Moore was transferred to the New York office and Dick Erb went to Caneel Bay as General Manager. Jim Reed stayed on as Butterfield's Executive Assistant.

At the time, Mr. B's and Bobbye Hughes' biggest marketing problem was combatting the rumor that the Hotel was always full. They ran a simple, clever ad campaign that showed the September calendar with available dates circled. When those filled, they moved on to October. By November, there were not enough dates to bother advertising.

That same year, at the urging of Allston Boyer, Mr. Rockefeller formed a company, Rockresorts, to manage his hotels. Butterfield says, "Before that, Rockresorts was just a pile of papers on Allston Boyer's desk." His projects were diverse and widespread, but his standards were very high and very demanding. The creation of Rockresorts Incorporated would consolidate the management effort and insure consistent quality. Richard Holtzmann was named President, and nobody was better, and no hotel company could touch them.

In 1967, LSR and the Dillingham Corporation formed Dilrock Company, to develop properties on nearby lands leased by Parker Ranch or held under an agreement with the Queen Emma Estate. They intended to move forward with LSR's original plans for a hotel overlooking Hapuna Bay, several hundred residential condominiums, a subdivision of vacation homes an industrial complex and a village of affordable housing near Kawaihae.

Only a few months later, Eastern Air Lines obtained 60% ownership of Mauna Kea Beach Hotel in a stock negotiation, making LSR Eastern's majority stockholder. The airline company planned to join Dilrock in developing 5,000-10,000 acres over the next fifty years, beginning the expansion of the entire Kohala Coast into a major multiple resort area.

Although a lot of guests had doubts about the slightest change in their beloved beach retreat, Rockresorts maintained an "agreement of operations" with Eastern and it was business as usual. "Usual" of course had finer connotations to Rockresorts than to commoner hotel companies.

Among other strict LSR directives, nothing was placed in the Hotel anywhere without thoughtful consideration. And once placed, nothing was permitted to change without a design consultation. As one example, Rockresorts had a full-time "light-inspector," a woman named Leslie Wheel, for all their properties. She visited the hotels on a rotating schedule, but was never seen in daylight. After the sun went down she changed into dark clothes and slipped around the grounds making sure the lights were where they were supposed to be, of the proper low voltage, and unobtrusive but adequate. LSR used to say, "The lighting slips around. You have to keep it the way it's supposed to be." That was his thinking on everything. It had to be the best, and stay that way.

LSR's restaurants followed the same process. When Mauna Kea first opened, the well water from Waimea was a little discolored. The restaurants used heavy water glasses with a little yellow tint to them. Later, on one of LSR's property tours, he noticed clear, less expensive glasses on the tables.

He didn't yell; he never yelled. But the person who made that decision knew it was a mistake. Everything was the best there was and everything was there for a reason. You didn't just change things arbitrarily and Mr. Rockefeller did not hesitate to remind people of that fact. Mr. Butterfield and his staff took LSR's original intentions to the next level; they established policies which became traditions, and allowed tradition to grow into the Mauna Kea culture.

This was particularly true in the dining rooms. Chef Blum's luncheon buffet became legendary fast. It was an elaborate spread decorated with huge tropical flower arrangements and ice sculptures, like a banquet for royalty. Every day busloads of visitors stopped there on tours between Kona and Hilo.

In the Pavilion, Chef Blum and his staff of twenty (half Europeans, half Hawai'i residents) developed a ten-day cycle of rotating dinner menus, each one featuring a different international cuisine. It was unique in the industry. He used to say he changed the menus instead of the guests because they stayed so long (two or three weeks on average).

Between the fish and meat courses, they served an intermezzo or refresher dish called "Spoom." This light blend of Italian meringue and sherbet (lemon or pineapple, sometimes papaya) and laced with good Champagne, was prepared daily by Pastry Chef Klaus Limberg. Considered exotic and elegant, it became a trademark of Mauna Kea dining.

In the mornings, half the guests preferred to take breakfast on their lanai, so Chef Blum made his staff into "Room Service specialists." He sent up eggs and bacon in metal warmers and juice in glasses nested in crushed ice. Hot food stayed hot, and cold juice cold, without being diluted by ice. Smiling waitresses set the *lanai* with a tablecloth, polished silverware and fresh flowers.

It was LSR who brought up the whole issue of toast. It could be a long walk from the kitchen to the guest room and he was concerned that the toast would arrive cold on the plate, or soggy in the warmer. Guests were entitled to have their bread toasted light, medium or dark, exactly to their preference. The solution was to send individual electric toasters up with the breakfast trays. He had Mr. B install outlets on every *lanai,* expressly for that purpose.

This perfectionist attention to detail was at work in every area of the hotel, including the shops, which Mrs. Charlot Butterfield ran at a very high standard. She decided, after consultation with the company, to move the original beauty salon and barbershop from the Flower Court into a lower-traffic area, reasoning that women wouldn't mind a little bit longer walk to have their hair done, and men, apparently, didn't bother much with haircuts on vacation. They were replaced by a men's clothing shop and an art gallery.

Charlot traveled extensively, and filled the Gallery with unique handcrafted imports and antiques, and the work of Hawai'i's best artists. She brought in Madge Tennant, Lloyd Sexton, Luis Phol, Guy Buffet and many others. Honolulu artist and friend John Young, who had painted a mural for her at Hana Maui, had paintings there as well.

Mauna Kea's best known work of art, the great granite Buddha, arrived not long after the Butterfield's in 1967. It was one of four that were positioned North, South, East and West around a "tank," a pond in southeast India. Davis Allen secured one for Mr. Rockefeller; one went to the Art Institute in Chicago, one remained and one disappeared. Mr. Butterfield coordinated the arrival of the statue from New York, with the arrival of its granite base from Canada. He arranged for a Buddhist priest from the town of Honoka`a to conduct a blessing.

Mr. Rockefeller was fascinated by the image of the Buddha. He collected statues and arranged them in his office and his home, including in the bathroom, and he had sited the location of this Buddha very, very carefully. It was extremely important that it be properly placed the first time.

It was a dark, rainy day. Mr. Butterfield and his Chief Engineer Derrick Cockle decided to bury a time capsule under the huge stone base. Derrick cut the top off a #10 can and they put in a copy of the day's newspapers, *Time* magazine, a copy of the Union contract and assorted unremembered small items. They buried it just before the Priest arrived. He said some words over the statue while it was still in the crate and then he left without much more to-do. When Mr. B and his engineer opened the crate, they saw the Buddha had a broken nose.

It wasn't that serious, some unaccounted-for shipping damage, which had been repaired in New York before the statue was shipped. It was noticeable, but it didn't detract from the Buddha's serenity in the least. He began his long meditation at the top of the grand staircase and never told anyone how it happened.

Alika, the Hotel's resident Scarlet Macaw, lived inside a work of art, a nine-foot tall brass cage on the Promenade level, just outside the gift shop. Originally, the empty cage was only a decoration. The "bird garden" was a collection of ornate wirework cages on the Lobby level, where pairs of finches, canaries and other small tropical birds chirped greetings to passing guests.

So many people asked about the big empty cage however, that Mr. B decided to fill it. Alika (short for Alexander the Great according to one source) came from a Mr. Marvin Devereux, who got him, his brother Laka and sister Mumu from a Mr. Hiroshi Tagami in Kahaluu, Oahu. Devereux hand-fed the babies, and took them to work with him at the First National Bank in Honolulu. When they got too big for the cardboard box, he decided to sell them.

At the tender age of four and a half months, Alika flew over to the Big Island (on a plane) in Devereux's lap and immediately established his rule of the roost, which he maintained for the next thirty years. Although most of his time was spent behind bars, he did occasionally roam around on the floor, and sometimes ventured up into the lobby. He was particular about his friends, and partial to women. While he allowed the shop ladies to baby him day and night, more than one finger of a groundskeeper, engineer or executive (including general manager) carries a scar from that big black beak.

{For the many readers who have asked, Alika boarded at a private home (this writer's) while Mauna Kea was closed for renovation 1994-96. During that time, probably out of boredom according to the veterinarian, she started plucking out her own feathers. Dr. Betsy Webb, while trying various treatments for the behavior, had Alika tested and determined she was a female after all. Although Alika improved enough to come back to work for a short time, she wasn't able to break the habit completely and stay in shape for the job. She retired to Dr. Webb's office in Kona.

One day two women came to visit. They were mother and daughter who had stayed at Mauna Kea many times. The daughter always loved Alika, who would sit on her arm and let her pet her head. Once when she was a little girl, she found Alika outside her cage and tried to pick her up as usual. Alika took a nip at the little girl's toe. When she ran to her mother in the Lobby, Alika followed her all the way upstairs. To the amazement of mother and daughter, Alika rubbed her head against the girl's injured foot and said "Sorry." As it turns out the two women eventually moved to Maui where they raised other large birds. They very much wanted Alika to join the family and flew her to her new home on her third island the next day. Although she recently passed away, her story had a happy ending.}

The original plan for Mauna Kea was to add more rooms in several stages, if the hotel was as successful as everyone dreamed. In 1968, the company decided to go ahead with construction of the Beachfront wing and a second dinner restaurant, The Batik. Skidmore Owings Merrill passed on the job and Wimberly, Whisenand, Allison, Tong and Goo signed on as architects. Honolulu expert Phyllis Brownlee did the interior decoration of guest rooms in a South Pacific style and incorporated original John Young paintings in each room. John Young later donated his beautiful "Horses" to the library/television lounge named after him.

The Batik was intended to capture the romance and mystique of the Orient. The upper level resembled a "houdah," the royal platform which carried an emperor in procession. Appointed with Indonesian batik wallhangings, high-backed wicker chairs and whimsical terra cotta animal figures, the Batik was romantic with a distinctive air of class. The menu featured exotic curries and elegant tableside services such as Caesar Salad and flambéed desserts. Naturally, a second kitchen was added and Chef Albert Dideriks stepped up to oversee the operation, and maintain it as one of the best in Hawai'i.

In 1973, the Queen Kaahumanu Highway was built linking Mauna Kea and the Kawaihae area to Kona Airport. LSR was instrumental in the project, working closely with Hawai'i County. That same year, Rockresorts added even more guest rooms by placing the eighth floor on top of the main building, with the hotel in full operation. The building was basically three separate pieces, and the eighth floor bridged two of them like icing on a cake. An earthquake in the finishing stages shook the "icing" lose, and shifted the new floor several inches. In spite of this, and construction noise, dust and other inconveniences, guests continued to enjoy the Mauna Kea, and to pay the going rate, as if nothing could possibly go wrong.

Thanks to far-reaching, excellent and artistic planning, along with the perfection of place and time, the hotel ran successfully high occupancy for many years. Facilities expanded to include a new tennis center and a luxury catamaran, the Kamehameha, for snorkeling, sunset and moonlight sails. A waiting list grew for the holiday period, with celebrities and who's who's competing for the better rooms. Gabby Hayes and Bing Crosby loved the golf course. Alfred Hitchcock, Lucille Ball, Kirk Douglas, Sander Vonocur, James Stewart, Carol Burnett, Julie Andrews, Danny Kaye, Joel Gray, Ed McMahon, Phil Donahue and Marlo Thomas, Jim Nabors, Paul Anka, Bobby Vinton, Gene and Majel Roddenberry, William Shatner, Carl Sagan, Robert

Adi with Arte Johnson and his wife Gisela

Mondavi, Julio Gallo, Arte and Gisela Johnson, Danielle Steele and her family and many other celebrities were frequent guests.

A hotel that successful can establish and adhere to certain policies that are almost laughable in today's hospitality business. They charged an advance deposit of three day's room rate, not refundable with less than two week's notice. Only twin beds were provided and only three persons could occupy a room with a rollaway bed or crib but not both; a family of four was required to take two rooms. Travel agent and airline discounts (33 1/3%) were only available from May to November. Levels of dress codes prevailed: jackets at dinner, whites on the tennis courts, proper golf attire, beach coverups in all public areas, and absolutely no rubber slippers. And, they did not accept credit cards.

Staffing was almost one-to-one (employee to guest); nobody talked about labor dollars. Employee handbooks were entitled "The Importance of a Guest" and "The Value of a Smile." Full-property training was mandatory. LSR disliked the commercial feeling of arrows and directional signage. Guests were supposed to ask where things were, and employees were expected to know. Service was not just a word.

More tangible Rockefeller touches were put in place for a reason and became unchallenged tradition. The plumeria *lei* greeting. Macadamia nuts at the Copper Bar, *taro* chips at the Gazebo, sizzling *pupus* on individual hibachis. Monogrammed towels, custom shampoo, loofah sponges and live orchid plants in the eighth floor baths. Logo playing cards for bridge on rainy days. Three-tiered petits fours trays presented after dinner with the pink, green and white mac nut chocolates. The warm pastry tray passed during breakfast. Spoom. The hot popcorn machine on movie nights, and the hot dog cart at the beach. Dinner jackets and dancing on the Batik Terrace. A stroll down the path to watch the manta rays dance. None of these things meant anything by itself. Altogether, they were Mauna Kea memories, and the guests couldn't get enough of them.

This is the place that welcomed "Mr. Mauna Kea" and his family on July 10, 1973. He began as Manager under Bob Butterfield and he was perfect for the job. European-trained and impeccably presented, Adi Kohler immediately stood for something. His experience put him at ease with people from everywhere, at every level of society, and he was not afraid of difficult situations. He did what Rockefeller did. He hired the best people he could find, asked their advice and listened to it. He treated people like human beings and let them do their jobs.

He treated change with respect. He was the right man in the right place at the right time.

Five years later in 1978, Mr. Rockefeller sold the Mauna Kea to UAL, Inc., parent company of United Airlines, Hertz and Western International Hotels, which later became Westin Hotels & Resorts. The initial purchase included the golf course and some undeveloped lands adjacent to Hapuna Beach State Park and along the Queen Kaahumanu Highway, for a purchase price of $18.6 million. By December of 1979, Mauna Kea Properties (the land company established to develop residential real estate) was included in the package.

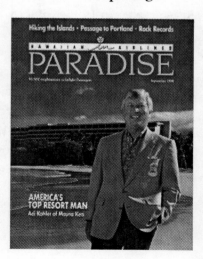

The negotiations between Mr. Rockefeller and Richard Holtzmann of Rockresorts and the corporate officers of UAL included a personal request that the Mauna Kea always be operated according to LSR's benchmark of excellence. They selected a team of people who could uphold those high standards, such professionals in the industry as Eddie Carlson and Dick Ferris with UAL, and Harry Mullikin, Lynn Himmelman and Bill Hewlett with

Western. The company moved Bob Butterfield up to Managing Director and promoted Adi Kohler to General Manager of Mauna Kea Beach Hotel. For ten years, their ultimately successful mission was to keep Mauna Kea at her peak performance.

In 1988, Kohler was named Resort Executive of the Year by the American Hotel & Motel Association at its 77th annual meeting in Dallas. He was the first Hawai'i hotelier to receive such national recognition. That same year, Mauna Kea was sold to the very prosperous Seibu Railway Corporation, who ran the popular Prince Hotel chain in Japan. Owned by one of the wealthiest men in the world, Seibu was among the very few companies with the resources to develop the resort property in its totality. The agreement left Westin to manage Mauna Kea until 1991, when it would become an independent operation, establishing the first of several Prince Hotels in Hawai'i. Plans were already underway to construct Hapuna Golf Course, Hapuna Beach Prince Hotel and additional residential properties.

In July of 1994, the Mauna Kea closed for a renovation while Hapuna prepared to open. Mauna Kea Golf Course, the 19th Hole restaurant and the Gazebo Bar on the beach at Kauna'oa Bay remained open. The statue of Buddha went back in his crate for a while, to protect him from damage during construction. When Mauna Kea re-opened in December of 1995, Kohler was named Managing Director of Mauna Kea Resort under a five-year contract to continue his leadership, and to maintain and strengthen relationships with employees, homeowners, club members and the Big Island community. The Mauna Kea Beach Hotel, a place of timeless quality for generations of guests year after year, had become the cornerstone of Mauna Kea Resort Community, along with Hapuna Beach Prince Hotel and a growing village of private residences and vacation homes.

Adi Kohler retired on June 30, 2000. He'd gotten a little too tall for the ceiling. In September of that year, he hit a hole-in-one on Number Three.

NOTES

The title of this book comes from countless comments from guests who heard my life story and said, "Adi, you have to write a book. You are Mr. Mauna Kea." I'd like to thank everyone who said this over the twenty-seven years with the Resort, and all of our guests and friends from Jackson Lake Lodge, Caneel Bay, Dorado Beach, the DaVinci Hotel and Mauna Kea.

English is my third language, and therefore it would have been very challenging for me to write a book on my own. Cathey Tarleton listened to my story and put it into proper words. *Mahalo nui loa.*

A.W.K.

Secretary/author Cathey Tarleton with the Boss

Adi W. Kohler,
Bailli-Commandeur, 2000

Kristin and Christian Kohler, Bieni and
Bob Johnson

Ryan and Alicia Johnson

Alexander and Elyse Kohler

Bibliography

Don Aanavi, *The Art of Mauna Kea,* the East-West Center and
Mauna Kea Beach Hotel, 1989

Abraham K. Akaka, "Remarks at the Dedication Luncheon of the
Mauna Kea Beach Hotel," the Island of Hawaii, Saturday, July 24,
1965

Jim Becker, "Jim Becker's Hawaii," *Honolulu Star-Bulletin,* December 20, 1966

Cobey Black, "Rockefeller's Regal Roost," *Paradise of the Pacific,*
July/August 1965. "Who's News," *Honolulu Star-Bulletin,* April
1965

John M. Black, "The Renewal of Mauna Kea Beach Hotel," *Hawaii
Hospitality,* February-March, 1996

Joseph Brennan, *The Parker Ranch of Hawaii,* The John Day
Company, New York, 1974

Gwilym S. Brown, "A Shocking Approach to Tranquility," *Sports
Illustrated*, July 28, 1965

Berry Boxold, "He Serves Spoom...," *Honolulu Star-Bulletin,* May
25, 1966

Robert Butterfield, interview over lunch at the Koa House Grille,
June 4, 2002

Eddie Carlson, *Reflections of a Lucky Fellow*

Bill Cook, "The Things That Make Hawaii Different," *New York
Times, November 7, 1965*

Lesley Downer, *The Brothers: The Hidden World of Japan's
Richest Family,* Random House, 1995

Gary Paul Gates, "Laurance Rockefeller — A View with a Room,"
Venture Magazine, March 1969

Karen Horton, "Adi Kohler," *Hawaii Hospitality*, Summer 1987

Maxine C. Hughes, "MKB Dedication - A Memory And Conversation
Topic," *Hawaii-Tribune Herald,* August 8, 1965

Richard Joseph, "The Three Greatest Hotels in the World," *Esquire*,
December 1967

Bill Kwon, "Grand Designer Returns to Mauna Kea," *Honolulu Star-
Bulletin*, December 16, 1989

Sheree Lipton, "Man of Mauna Kea," *Hawaiian Airlines Paradise*,
    September 1988
Jeremy Main, "Host to the Relaxing Rich," *Money,* May 1975
Leavitt Morris, "Travel Editor's Diary," *The Christian Science
    Monitor,* December 14, 1965
Howard Pierce "Already New Mauna Kea Beach Hotel Is Almost A
    Kamaaina," and "Mauna Kea Beach Hotel Closely Linked With
    History," *Hawaii Tribune-Herald,* August 8, 1965
Ken Polsson, "Chronology of World War II," ww.islandnet.com/
    ~kpolsson/ww2hist/, April 2002
Caroyln Rice, "Puerto Rico's sister Resorts Offer a Two-for-One
    Experience," *Travel Agent,* November 3, 1997,
    www.findarticles.com
Laurance S. Rockefeller, "Remarks at the Dedication Luncheon of
    the Mauna Kea Beach Hotel," the Island of Hawaii, Saturday, July
    24, 1965
Robert Shea, "Fasching," www.serve.com/shea/germusa/
    karneval.htm, May 2002
A.P. Wall, "Tourism's the Thing - From Hilo to Kohala," *Honolulu
    Advertiser, July 12, 1965*
Robin Winks, *Laurance S. Rockefeller, Catalyst for Conservation,*
    Island Press, 1997
Hal Wood, "The Monster of Mauna Kea," *Honolulu Star-Bulletin*,
    March 14, 1965

Un-credited articles and internet sources:
"Bayerischer Hof," www.orbitz.com, May 2002
Chicago Architects Oral History Project, interview with Edward
    Charles Bassett, January 30-February 1, 1989, www.artic.edu/
    aic/collections/dept_architecture/bassett.html
*Hawaii Tribune-Herald, Honolulu Star-Bulletin and Honolulu
    Advertiser,* various articles (no byline) 1965-67
"History," www.hotelhanamaui.com, May 2002
"History," www.caneelbay.com, May 2002
"History," www.littledixbay.com, May 2002
"History & Annals," www.steigenberger.com, May 2002

"Hotel de Crillon Paris," http://miseajour.apicius.com/crillon/uk/
    il.asp, May 2002
"Hotel Fürstenhof Bad Pyrmont,"
    www.fuerstenhof.steigenbereger.com
"Robert Trent Jones Sr., " http:/print.infoplease.com/ipa/
    A0873366.html, The Learning Network, November 2001
Raffles Hotel Vier Jahreszeiten, www.raffles.com/vier.htm, May
    2002
"Splendor and Decadence," Bavaria Alpine Net Guide,
    www.bavaria.com/travel, May 2002
"Sudetes," "Munich Pact," "Czechoslovakia,"
    www.encyclopedia.com, May 2002
"World War Two 1939-1946 Chronology," www.simonides.org/
    links/wars
"World War Two in Europe," www.historyplace.com/worldwar2/
    timeline/ww2time.htm

LaVergne, TN USA
18 March 2010
176444LV00002B/44/A